"There's No Better Place Than Here"

"There's No Better Place Than Here"
Social Change in Three Newfoundland Communities

Ralph Matthews

Peter Martin Associates Limited

Canadian Cataloguing in Publication Data

Matthews, David Ralph, 1943–
"There's no better place than here"

(Canadian experience series)

Bibliography: p.
ISBN 0-88778-135-7 bd. ISBN 0-88778-136-5 pa.

1. Newfoundland – Social conditions – Case studies.
2. Newfoundland – Economic conditions – Case studies.
I. Title. II. Series.

HN110.N4M38 309.1'718 C76–017051–7

Peter Martin Associates Limited
35 Britain Street, Toronto, Canada M5A 1R7

United Kingdom: Books Canada, 1 Bedford Road, London N2
United States: Books Canada, 33 East Tupper St., Buffalo, N.Y. 14203

Acknowledgements

The data on the three communities described in this book were collected while I was a research fellow in the Institute of Social and Economic Research, Memorial University of Newfoundland. I wish to thank the Institute and its former director, Robert Paine, for their support of my work.

I would also like to thank my research assistants Roger Down and Patrick Kavanagh for their help in compiling background data on the three communities and for their assistance in interviewing some of the residents.

I am grateful to Sandra Wallman for encouraging me to submit a proposal for this book after only a chance conversation, and for her continuing support through several long delays. I am similarly indebted to Carol and Peter Martin of Peter Martin Associates for their acceptance of this work at such an early stage.

However, as with most social research, my greatest debt is to the people described in this book—the people of the three communities studied. I hope that my study will encourage planners to devise viable and vital ways of life so that these people and others like them can continue to live "the good life" in their home communities. It is my hope that they will gain more than they lose from this intrusion on their privacy.

My wife, Anne, encouraged me to write and comforted me in my frustrations. This book is dedicated to her.

Note

The real names of the communities described in this book have been changed to protect the anonymity of my informants. For the same reason some of the names of nearby communities have also been changed and the accompanying geographic details have been slightly altered.

To Anne

CONTENTS

INTRODUCTION TO THE
CANADIAN EXPERIENCE SERIES

Each of the monographs in this Series deals with a particular aspect of Canadian society and is based on professional research in one of the social sciences. The editors and publishers of Canadian Experience designed the Series to meet two particular needs. One is the need for inexpensive and readable accounts of life in Canada, produced under entirely Canadian auspices but available to readers outside Canada as well as in this country. The other is the need for clear and unpretentious statements of the assumptions and processes underlying professional social research—information which is essential to beginning students of the social sciences and of increasing relevance to the general reader.

Two features of the Series may be noted in this respect. First, each of the books will include, as this one does, an explicit and unusually detailed statement of research methods and methodology. This appears in every case as a separate section or chapter, so that the body of the work which follows, although necessarily structured by the author's approach, may be left free of unexplained concepts and professional jargon, and so that students may see clearly that a method of research can be described or assessed only in relation to the context of research and the problem with which it is concerned. Teachers of social science at all levels know that accounts of what social scientists do are meaningless unless all three facets—method, context and problem—are related and presented together.

Second, the work behind the titles in Canadian Experience is not the product of one single professional discipline. Recent trends indicate that the boundaries between the various social sciences are becoming less rigid and less useful. No scientific discipline can now afford to restrict itself to a single theoretical framework: approaches vary within single institutions and cross and re-cross the boundaries of university departments. While a variety of approaches to social research are presented in this Series, the variation does not necessarily tally with professional labels—although the professional calibre of each writer is established and his or her affiliation specified where it is relevant. We would hope and expect that each volume will be of interest along a gamut of social scientific persuasions as well as outside academic circles.

This Series is both more eclectic and methodologically more specific than has been usual at this level. Its focus on studies of Canada could be justified simply on the grounds that many Canadians are now demanding new dimensions to their national identity: they want to know what it means to be a Canadian. But we are also convinced that the vitality and variety of the "Canadian experience" has been consistently underestimated, and that these monographs on Canadian society and research offer insights into situations and social processes which are significant to us all.

—Sandra Wallman
General Editor

Preface

Ever since Canada was founded, Canadians have been in retreat—a retreat from the land and from the sea. They may retain the grass roots myth, the myth of growing up on farms and in small fishing villages, but few of them ever did. By 1920 over half of all Canadians lived in cities. Today nearly 80 percent do, and the drive for urbanization has concentrated them in a very few centres. In 1971 the fifteen largest metropolitan areas in Canada contained 50 percent of the population. Although Canada occupies the second largest land mass in the world, Canadians have become a nation of urbanites.

Urbanization has become so much a part of Canadian life that most now take it for granted. To most Canadians it seems natural that they must live in large cities in order to have jobs. It seems normal that industries grow in the "golden horseshoe" around Lake Ontario, and do not fare as well in either the fertile soil of the Prairies or on the barren craigs of the Maritimes. If occasionally some urban Canadians look with longing at life in the smaller towns and cities, their longing is usually combined with the knowledge that they have opportunities which are not possible in such communities.

This book is about those other Canadians who refuse to accept the urban dream and the industrial goal. It focuses on those left behind in the retreat from rural areas. It highlights their plea for viable rural settings which will enable them to remain where they are rather than force them into urban centres.

This book is about Newfoundland which, since joining Canada in 1949, has experienced a faster rate of urbanization than any other area of the country. Although the stereotypical Newfoundlander is still the fisherman living in a remote village, nearly 60 percent of the population now lives in urban areas. The rush towards urbanization has been brought about through the direct encouragement and involvement of both the Government of Newfoundland and the Government of Canada. Both have sponsored programmes of community relocation designed to shift the population from small rural communities to large industrial centres.

In less direct ways government has been involved in the urbanization of other areas of Canada. The original reasons for industries to settle in southern Ontario have all but disappeared. New industries now locate there in order to be near other industries and because the people themselves have moved there to find work. This *self-fulfilling prophecy of industrialization and urbanization* is encouraged by government freight and transportation policies which help sustain these metropolises and maintain the hinterland status of much of the east and west. It is further enhanced by deliberate government attempts to reduce Canadian farmers and fishermen to one-quarter of their present number within the next generation. Therefore, although my study focuses on Newfoundland, it has implications for the development of every region in the country.

"There's No Better Place Than Here" is about the few and not about the many. Those who are content with an urban way of life are likely to consider it biased. They will argue that it glorifies a way of life which is no longer desirable. To the extent that rural life involves extreme hardship, I would agree with them. I would also agree that life in the three communities described in this book is often brutal and harsh. But the ever-increasing size of our cities and the problems associated with them also leave much to be desired. I believe that it is time for us to end the programmes and policies which reduce Canada's rural areas and outlying regions to the status of exploited hinterlands, the suppliers of raw materials and people. Canadians should be concerned with fostering a variety of ways of living and with exploring ways of raising the standard of life in rural communities so that they will become viable places in which to live.

. . . Every Canadian has a right to the good life, whatever the province or community he lives in. . . .

—Pierre Elliott Trudeau,
   "The Practice and Theory of Federalism",
   Federalism and the French Canadians

CHAPTER I

THE OTHER SIDE OF PLANNING: PROBLEMS AND METHODOLOGICAL PROCEDURES

Twenty-seven years ago Newfoundland became Canada's tenth province. For Newfoundland it was a union of necessity. Centuries of British colonial mismanagement followed by decades of local political corruption had drained her of more resources than her one commodity, the fishery, could provide (Great Britain, 1933; Noel, 1971; Matthews, 1974). A small local elite had become rich, but most Newfoundlanders in 1949 were living in rural rishing villages where they were totally dependent on the precarious fortunes of the erratic inshore fishery and the good graces of the village merchant. With the exception of two paper mills and some small mines, there were virtually no industries in the island province. Standards of living were low. Educational facilities were poor. Roads were almost nonexistent. Hospitals were widely scattered. Social assistance in time of need was meagre. Most Newfoundlanders were living a peasant existence much as their forefathers had done for generations.

The leader of the movement to unite Newfoundland with Canada, and the province's premier for the first twenty-three years of Confederation, was Joseph R. Smallwood. He set as his goal the social and economic development of the province to equal standards of living in other parts of Canada. But not all Newfoundlanders were willing to accept the cornucopia of delights which Smallwood offered. Although they lived in poverty, many were unwilling to give up independent rural life for existence in an urban centre and work in a factory. Yet in order to have a twentieth-century standard of living, this is exactly what was required of them.

In 1949 Newfoundland had close to 1,500 rural communities, most of which had fewer than 300 residents. Many of these communities were isolated on islands or on inaccessible stretches of Newfoundland's 6,000-mile coastline. The cost of providing roads and other services to many of them was prohibitive. Rather than simply providing these facilities in urban and semi-urban centres and letting Newfoundlanders move to them as they saw fit, the Newfoundland government inaugurated an extensive

1

programme of community centralization. Ostensibly this programme was
designed to help people who wanted to move to more favourable centres
but were unable to afford the costs involved (Lane, 1967). Its actual goal
was to relocate entire remote communities: assistance was provided only
if 100 percent of a community's residents certified their willingness to
move. As might be expected, this feature of the programme entailed
group pressures and sometimes the intimidation of those who had no
particular desire to move. The common process of rural to urban population drift was transformed into a community-wide mass phenomenon.

In 1965 a revised version of this programme was inaugurated under
joint federal-provincial sponsorship. This time the specific goal was declared to be the complete evacuation of 600 communities and the relocation of 70,000 people in selected "growth centres" (*Daily News,* November 6, 1968). Through wide publicity, increased financial incentives and
effective organization this programme achieved remarkable "success".
Between 1953 and 1965 the provincial programme had evacuated only
115 communities containing 7,500 persons (Lane, 1967: 564). In its
first five years the revised programme closed 119 communities and relo-
cated 16,114 occupants (Government of Newfoundland, no date).

As a consequence of these two programmes, most rural Newfoundlanders found themselves in a dilemma. While life in urbanized areas
offered some attractions, those affected knew that the land and the sea
could at least provide them and their families with the necessities of food,
shelter and clothing. Few of the adult generation had the skills or the
education which would enable them to find permanent, well-paying jobs
in an urban, industrial environment. For them life in even the smaller
towns meant a few months or years of back-breaking labour, followed by
long periods of unemployment and welfare.

At the same time it was obvious to many rural Newfoundlanders that
the future of their home communities was bleak. In most areas the fish
stocks were declining and it became more and more difficult to wrest an
adequate living from the sea. Given the government's policy, they and
their families could have the comforts and amenities of modern life
only by moving to larger centres. Only there could their children get the
education they would need in future years.

Faced with this dilemma, thousands chose to resettle. The resettlement process has been the subject of several studies, including two by
this writer (Iverson & Matthews, 1968; Matthews, 1970; Robb & Robb,
1969; Copes, 1972). Most of these studies emphasized the difficult social,

economic and psychological adjustments which had to be made by those who moved. All focused on people and communities which had already moved and examined, only indirectly, the way of life that existed prior to resettlement. Little is known about the conditions which led people to move. While many resettled, thousands more, presumably faced with the same pressures, chose not to. Yet their communities had changed too, and those who chose to remain in them had to adjust. This book is a study of the ways in which these people who did *not* move to urban areas withstood and adapted to the pressures of change.

The Three Communities

The process of change can be investigated on several levels. At the most general level one can collect and analyse province-wide data on trends in employment and unemployment, occupational composition, population movements, births, deaths and the numerous other statistics which depict and describe a complex society. This is done in Chapter II and it demonstrates that Newfoundland in general and rural Newfoundland in particular, face a very real social and economic crisis.

But an analysis at this level provides only a backdrop and contributes little to an understanding of the way people adapt to the pressures of change. To understand this one must observe and talk with the people themselves. With this in mind I spent part of 1970 and 1971 in three remote Newfoundland communities. In each of these communities I interviewed large segments of the adult population. The data gathered in this fashion form the core of this book for they show how Newfoundlanders have faced and continue to deal with the forces of change.

All three communities are small, with populations ranging from 200 to 700 people. While change has occurred in these communities in the past fifty years, the way of life in each still retains its traditional character. Most families obtain their basic livelihood from the smallboat inshore fishery, and supplement it with vegetables from the kitchen garden and firewood and timber from the family woodlot. All three communities were chosen for study precisely because they remain traditional despite their proximity to large centres of commercial or industrial activity. Even though they are exposed to the pulls of urban living, they appear to have maintained a viable rural life. Most importantly, they have resisted all efforts to encourage them to resettle.

There were also more specific reasons for choosing each of these three communities. Small Harbour, one of the English-speaking communities, is located on an offshore island and at the time it was studied had neither electricity nor regular boat connections with the mainland. Its only direct contact was the approximately bi-weekly coastal boat service during the summer and fall period when the bay was ice-free. Although Small Harbour was the smallest (192 people), most isolated and least serviced of the communities studied, it was the only community in all of Newfoundland to issue a public statement that it would not be forced into resettling. Therefore it appeared to be an ideal place to study how rural people attempt to maintain their traditional way of life in the face of pressures to change.

Mountain Cove, the other English-speaking community studied, is relatively large (689 people) and has been connected by road to nearby communities for nearly a decade. Although it is in one of the most scenic areas of the province, a territory slated to become a national park, residents of neighbouring communities think Mountain Cove has a low standard of living and it is isolated socially. For a number of reasons the original proposals for the park specified that the community be evacuated by 1979. When I arrived to conduct my research (summer 1970), the residents still felt the threat of resettlement.

The third community, Grande Terre, represents Newfoundland's small French-speaking population and is almost unknown to other Newfoundlanders. Little about its origins and virtually nothing about its culture can be found in print. Rumours abound about the residents' ferocity and lawlessness. Before going to the area I heard stories of battles with chain saws and of murders which had never been reported to the authorities. A government official responsible for the development of the area feared that he would be attacked if ever he left the safety of his car. Grande Terre's 402 people live at the end of a long, almost impassable gravel road which connects it to a nearby English-speaking community. Ten miles by sea and seventy miles by road from any other French community, its isolation is both cultural and physical. It provided an excellent vehicle for a comparative analysis of the effects of social change.

Methods of Data Collection

My method of obtaining information was the same in each of the three communities studied. Most researchers of small communities employ the method of participant observation: they simply live in a community and record the daily pattern of life around them. Usually they develop close friendships with selected community members who become their "key informants", interpreting local events as they see them. Those who use the participant observer method generally argue that it permits them to obtain in-depth insights into community life which would be impossible if they had not become trusted residents of the community. They claim that survey research methods are inclined to provide only superficial insights into predetermined questions and that the interviews and interviewers intimidate local residents who are unfamiliar with the sophisticated and impersonal ways of outsiders.

But my previous work in Newfoundland had made me acutely aware that one of the real dangers of community research is the often unwittingly biased nature of participant observation. Even the smallest community is divided on many issues, and those who are most vocal quickly seek out an outsider and attempt to win him over. This is particularly the case when the participant observer is seen as someone capable of dealing with outside authorities who are in a position to help the community. When this happens, even the observers' strongest assurances of objective neutrality are unlikely to convince community members who quickly jump to the conclusion that the purpose of his visit is connected with future government plans for the area. Local residents may join forces in an attempt to influence his observations. Even when this does not happen, an observer's field notes are quite likely to overrepresent some interests and to underrepresent others.

Even if the participant observer honestly believes that he has been able to maintain impartiality, he is unlikely to convince outsiders of this. Readers of his work may charge that his subjective approach makes his conclusions suspect. If his work also has policy implications, those whose vested interests are threatened by his report are likely to seize on this as a sure way of discrediting his findings.

To try to overcome these problems, I decided to adapt some form of representative sampling to the study of small community life. A representative sample is drawn in such a way that every person (or household) has an equal chance of being included. If I were to interview such a sample of informants, I would be able to generalize about the range of attitudes held throughout the whole community with reasonable assurance of being accurate. And I could not be accused of having deliberately confined my study to only one segment of the community.

To obtain a random sample, it is usually necessary to have a complete list of all the residents or households in the community being studied. Then it is a simple matter of selecting a sample by using a table of random numbers. The most widely-used lists of potential respondents are telephone directories and voters' lists. But there are few telephones in rural Newfoundland and, at the time of my study, the voters' list was more than five years out of date. A more accurate list was needed and, in the course of subsequent investigations, I learned that the Canadian post office annually publishes complete lists of all householders in Canada who live in areas not otherwise recorded by commercial city directories. This list contains the name and occupation of each household head.

Before drawing a random sample from those who can be described as the *general population,* I decided to structure my study in one further way to eliminate one of the common weakness of interview studies. Researchers generally interview the spouse who is at home when he or she calls. In Newfoundland where comparatively few women work and are thus available when the interviewer calls, there is a danger of over representing women. Because my previous studies had convinced me that Newfoundland is a tradition oriented society in which most of the final decisions on community affairs are made by men, I decided to omit from the general population listing those few women who were household heads.[1]

My original sample consisted of approximately half of the male household heads in Small Harbour and Grande Terre and a somewhat smaller proportion in Mountain Cove, due to the larger size of that community. I determined to stop interviewing only when I had called on all of the households in my original sample *and* when the information I received in later interviews was consistent with that received from earlier ones, indicating that there was little likelihood of obtaining much more general information about the community. In Small Harbour and Mountain Cove the replies of my original sample seemed so consistent that it did not seem necessary to interview more respondents to comprehend the process of social change which was taking place. However in Grande Terre I selected and interviewed a small additional random sample in

---

[1] Most of these women are widows with children. My previous research suggest that many of them are protected and assisted by the brother(s) of their deceased husband. Since their attitude toward the community is highly dependent on the satisfaction and attitudes of their brother(s)-in-law, little insight could be gained from including one or two of them in our sample.

order to obtain further information.[2] I personally conducted half of the interviews in each community, while the remainder were conducted by two Newfoundlanders, both graduate students in sociology.

While the general population sample would allow me to generalize about the attitudes and values of the community, previous studies had led me to realize that there are persons in every small community who hold positions of leadership and responsibility and who have more than average influence on its affairs. If I failed to contact these leaders, they might feel slighted and attempt to dissuade their followers from co-operating with me. In any case I was anxious to talk with all such persons because of their potential influence in effecting community change. My past experience indicated too, that it is the merchants in rural Newfoundland communities who most frequently fulfil these leadership functions, so I abstracted these names from the postal lists. This became my sample of *traditional leaders.*

A third group of residents whose views I was particularly anxious to obtain were those "charismatic people" who had risen to prominence simply through their personal qualities. To discover such persons, I asked every person interviewed whom he considered to be a leader in his community. Many of those mentioned were already in the sample of traditional leaders, while a few others had by chance been among those selected from the random sample of the general population. I decided to include as leaders all those charismatic persons who were mentioned by five or more community members, and I subsequently interviewed any such persons not already included in the original two groups.

Thus in each of the three communities I interviewed two groups of people. The first group was a random sample of the male household heads as selected from post office lists. The second group consisted of all of the community leaders as determined by both positional and reputational criteria. My research design then might be considered a form of "stratified random sampling". In a stratified sample the population is first

---

[2] Strict adherents to Popperian deduction may criticize my method and argue that it fails to fulfil the requirements for scientific generalization. They might point out that the very next interview in any of my communities could have contradicted my findings and led me to alter my interpretations. While this may be true, I would argue that I was engaged in a process of exploration and discovery and was in no position to formulate propositions prior to my study. (See Glazer and Strauss [1967] for a distinction between studies designed to generate theory and those designed to test theory.) I would also point out that the generalizations which I do make about the attitudes of the general population of any community are based on data obtained from a random sample of that population.

divided on the basis of certain preselected criteria and a sample is drawn
from each segment. My design differs primarily in that I interviewed all
of the persons designated as leaders by my criteria, rather than just a
sample of them. [3]

As the analysis which follows demonstrates, this design proved to be
highly workable and fortuitous. Throughout the community studies I
was able to generalize about the attitudes and values of the general population of each community and to compare these with the attitudes and
values of that community's leaders. In all three communities studied the
action (or inaction) of community leaders proved to be critically important in the process of change. My focus on leadership undoubtedly
helped me to better understand these changes.

The questionnaire which formed the basis of my interview with both
community leaders and members of the general population solicited information on a wide range of topics (see Appendix I). I have considerable
information on the standard of living of every respondent, his residential
and occupational mobility and the current residence of both his siblings
and children. At the community level, I solicited information on community leadership and organization, as well as information on recent
migration into and out of the community. Other questions probed the
extent of community co-operation and change and the degree of government pressure on community life. In addition the lengthy "Community
Satisfaction Index" (see Appendix II) provided a wide range of information
on the values of the people and their attitudes towards their community
and towards community change.

Before going to any of the three communities, I sent a letter to each
household head in my general sample and to each of the traditional
leaders, informing them that I would soon be calling on them and ex-
plaining in general terms the purpose of my study. Throughout the actual
process of interviewing and research, I was guided by the criteria underlying my research design. To ensure that women were not overrepresented
in my sample, I and the other interviewers made deliberate efforts to
interview male household heads. If the man of the house was not available when we first called, we arranged an appointment for a time when
he would be available. Because we were interviewing during the height
of the fishing season, we often had to make frequent calls on some homes
before we were able even to contact the household head to arrange a

---

[3] This was possible because of the relatively small size of this group.

later interview. While this methodology tended to overrepresent men, we were partially able to compensate by including in the interviews those wives who were present. Generally both husband and wife were together at the time of the interview.[4]

One of the major drawbacks of interviews is that the formal structure may limit the researcher to information on predetermined questions, and the interviewer may leave without ever becoming aware of important features of community life. To overcome this problem, my original questionnaire not only contained structured questions but also many open-ended ones which called for the general comments and opinions of the respondents on any subject that seemed relevant to our inquiry. In addition each interviewer recorded verbatim as many of the comments of the respondents as he possibly could. This included both the respondents' answers to the questions on the questionnaire, and their general comments and answers to any other questions which seemed relevant during the course of the interview.[5]

This approach to interviewing had two consequences. First, it generally resulted in more informal interviews than might seem apparent from the questionnaire. Second, it often produced quite lengthy interviews: many interviews lasted from two to three hours and became social occasions. We were frequently implored not to leave without "a cup of tea and something to eat". By the time most interviews ended there was little to suggest that they had been intimidating experiences for those interviewed.

This by no means exhausted my information on the three communities. Besides the interviews with the two sample groups, I also held lengthy conversations with a variety of other people who were familiar with each of the communities. These included clergymen, government officials and older residents who were able to supply a verbal local history. This information complements the more structured data.

[4]We formally interviewed a total of forty-four husbands and wives together, twelve single or widowed men, and nine married men separately. Even among this latter group many of the wives were present but refused to take part in the interview or chose to leave the room after a short interval.

[5]The community studies which follow contain many quotes from our respondents. These quotes are the actual verbatim comments of our respondents. I would add that, in some of the interviews which I personally conducted, I used a portable tape recorder. Whenever I did so I first obtained the respondent's permission to record what he said. I then turned on the tape recorder but continued also to write some of his answers on the questionnaire as I progressed through it. At a later date I transcribed the complete answers from the tapes to the questionnaires. Most of the people whose answers I taped seemed to quickly adjust to the fact that they were being recorded, and frequently ignored the unobtrusive tape recorder.

Framework of Analysis

The analysis of the material which follows will focus on two related aspects of social life. The first is the *structure* of community life in Newfoundland and the way that it is changing. In the course of its history every community develops a culture or way of doing things. Culture is to collective life what habits are to individual people. It is a way of doing things which has proven successful in the past and thus becomes the accepted and accustomed pattern. Culture also includes the accepted ways of relating to people. In every community some people are respected and come to hold leadership positions, while others receive lesser degrees of esteem and wield less power and influence.

Almost everywhere the traditional patterns of rural life are changing, and rural Newfoundland is no exception. Radio and television bring the outside world to the community, while roads allow community members increased access to the outside world. Community members with higher education and job opportunities now vie for power with established community leaders. Our data on community migration, leadership and co-operation provides an indication of the extent of these changes. Some changes are incorporated into the traditional way of life and actually serve to make it more viable. But other changes threaten the community's very existence.

Besides community structure, my second concern here is with the *attitudes and values* of the people who live in these communities. Values, as the word implies, are the principles which determine the choices people make—they are the bases upon which people choose their goals. In a rapidly changing world things which once were valued lose their importance and new ones take their place. Even the definition of what constitutes a good life changes.

There can be no doubt that most Newfoundlanders are no longer content to live the peasant existence of their forefathers. They now demand the comforts and amenities of modern life. To obtain these, some have been willing to give up much of their old way of living. But in the three communities I studied there is an obvious desire to mesh the old with the new. Most of those interviewed remain where they are because of their conviction that, *for them*, "There's no better place than here". From their perspective, the decision to remain where they are is more rational than to move to growth centres. My primary concern is to determine their reasons for this decision, and particularly to determine what it is about their current life that they value so much.

The implications of this analysis are far-reaching. While my immediate task is to examine three small communities, I also am trying to present the dilemma of the rural Newfoundlander and the rural Canadian faced with modernization, industrialization and social planning. As areas of "regional disparity" rural Newfoundland, and Atlantic Canada generally have been the subjects of much attention from development planners who are attempting to alter the process of social change which is occurring naturally in the area. In recent years most of the development plans in Canada have been influenced by the growth centre concept of development which favours the centralization of industry and population. This approach has been advocated by the Atlantic Provinces Economic Council as the strategy most suitable for the development of the Atlantic region (APEC, 1972). From its programmes, it appears that the federal Department of Regional Economic Expansion, too, has embraced the centralization approach.

It is therefore appropriate to examine the general strategies of development which affect the lives of the people of the Atlantic region. The way in which we selected our communities means that most of those we interviewed steadfastly oppose the changes which are planned for them. Their values are in direct opposition to many of the values of the planners, and the goals they have for their lives are quite different from those which the planners wish to thrust upon them. This enables us to see some of the basic conflicts over planning in the Atlantic region. Too often plans have been made without consideration of the lifestyles desired by many of the residents. While not everyone wishes to live a rural or semi-rural way of life, many still wish to do so. It is my belief that the first step towards good development planning should be a regard for the values and preferences of the people who are to be affected, and the subsequent incorporation of these values into policy planning whenever possible. Indeed it is largely this which separates planning from intimidation and coercion (Matthews, 1975b).

An Overview

Chapter II presents my analysis of the current social and economic plight of Newfoundland in general, and of rural Newfoundland in particular. Chapters III, IV and V examine each of the three sample communities in turn. A brief presentation of their history is followed by a discussion of their situation today, both in relation to the general development of Newfoundland and as it is seen through the eyes of the inhabitants. Finally, Chapter VI concludes with an analysis of the general strategies of development which affect the people of the Atlantic region, and a consideration of the relevance of our findings to them.

CHAPTER II

NEWFOUNDLAND'S SOCIAL AND ECONOMIC DEVELOPMENT PROBLEMS

In this chapter I will attempt to present the facts about Newfoundland which are relevant to any analysis of its social and economic change. But facts are always at the mercy of a frame of reference. Viewed from different perspectives they can be interpreted in quite different ways. Nowhere is this more apparent than when social planners and populace meet. The goals, values, training and life experience of each group may lead to strikingly different interpretations of existing information. In such a situation the sociologist has a unique opportunity to see things from both sides. His role is to use his expertise to interpret the available data in a manner useful to all parties (Matthews, 1975b). In the following pages I have attempted to do this, keeping in mind that my framework may at times blind me to more fruitful approaches.

Historical Notes

Although tens of thousands of fishermen came annually to fish Newfoundland's waters, almost none chose to settle. The usual explanation, that British laws prohibiting settlement in Newfoundland made permanent habitation virtually impossible, seems inadequate. These laws were enforced for only a few years (1633 to 1677), and even after their official repeal in 1811 there was no great surge of immigration. In 1857 over 91 percent of the population was native-born. Throughout her recorded history, Newfoundland has probably had fewer than 35,000 immigrants for the simple reason that around most of her ice-locked coast there was no work during the long winter months.

But because Newfoundlanders have been among the world's most prodigious producers of children the population of the province has grown rapidly. Between 1822 and 1874, the population quadrupled almost solely on the basis of natural increase (Rodgers, 1911:240).[1] By

---

[1] The natural increase of a population is the extent to which births exceed deaths.

1920 it had passed the quarter-million mark. Today there are more than half a million Newfoundlanders, over 96 percent of whom are native-born (see Table I).

The Depression of the 1930s severely affected Newfoundland. During that period up to 25 percent of the population received relief and the province's economy and government completely collapsed (Matthews, 1974). The Second World War was a boom to Newfoundland. It quickly became a strategic marshalling area for Atlantic convoys, and both the United States and Canada built several naval and air bases there. The war changed the whole character of Newfoundland. Men from every cove and hamlet worked in the construction and operation of the military bases where, particularly under the Americans, they learned valuable trades. At the end of the war Newfoundland had for the first time a nucleus of skilled urban workers and the basis of a stable economy. Before recession could set in again, Newfoundland joined Canada, and its skilled labourers were quickly put to work building the roads, schools, hospitals and other facilities needed to bring its living standard closer to that of the rest of Canada.

But while enormous gains have been made, the average income per person in Newfoundland during 1970 was only $1,784, compared to $3,092 for the rest of Canada and $3,584 in Ontario (Newfoundland, 1972:6). In addition Newfoundlanders have had to shoulder the highest cost of living in all of Canada. These statistics are symptoms of problems which lie deeply rooted in Newfoundland's social and economic structure.

Social and Economic Development Problems

The growth and dispersion of Newfoundland's population has been one of the province's most basic social and economic development problems. As one Newfoundland Royal Commission concluded, "Economic development embraces the whole socio-economic process whereby an economy's real income increases at a rate faster than its population growth" (Newfoundland, 1967:2-3). But in Newfoundland the population has tended to grow so rapidly that her economic gains have been largely lost.

The economic history of a country is often reflected in its birth rate. Newfoundland is no exception (see Tables 1 and 2). The high birth rate and low death rate which caused her population to surge during the nineteenth century continued into the twentieth century, and during the postwar "baby boom" the birth rate reached unprecedented levels. But just as the baby boom was ending elsewhere, Newfoundland joined Canada

Table 1

Population of Newfoundland and Labrador 1836-1971

Year	Population
1836	75,094
1857	124,288
1869	146,536
1874	161,374
1884	197,335
1891	202,040
1901	220,984
1911	242,619
1921	263,033
1935	289,588
1945	321,819
1951	361,416
1956	415,074
1961	457,853
1966	493,396
1971	522,104

Sources: *Census of Newfoundland and Labrador,* 1935, I: 9;
Thahane: *Population Growth and Shifts in Newfoundland;
Canada Year Book,* 1968, 1972.

and entered a new era of hope and prosperity. The Canadian government's family allowance system paid Newfoundlanders a "baby bonus" for every child, bringing scarce dollars into the traditional rural economy. As a result, in Newfoundland the baby boom of the 1940s continued well into the 1960s, giving the province the highest birth rate in Canada and close to the highest in North America.

The implications of this phenomenal rate of population growth for social and economic development are far-reaching. First, a large juvenile population means that a relatively small proportion of the population must support the rest. By 1966 over 51 percent of the population were in the 0-19 age group, while those over age 65 comprised another 5.9 percent. In 1968 less than 24 percent of the population was employed. Secondly, the high birth rate and large juvenile population has "eaten up"

Table 2

Newfoundland Live Birth, Death and Natural
Increase Rates per 1,000 Population by Periods, 1921 to 1971

Period	Average Live Birth Rate	Average Death Rate	Average Natural Increase Rate
1921 to 1925	26.7	14.0	12.7
1926 to 1930	25.1	13.7	11.4
1931 to 1935	23.4	12.8	10.6
1936 to 1940	25.8	12.4	13.4
1941 to 1945	29.8	11.8	18.0
1946 to 1950	36.2	9.3	26.9
1951 to 1955	34.1	7.6	26.5
1956 to 1960	34.6	7.2	27.4
1961 to 1965	31.5	6.6	24.9
1966 to 1970	25.8	6.2	19.6
1971	24.5	6.1	18.4

Sources: *Canada Year Book,* 1956, 1961, 1968, 1972;
            Vital Statistics, Preliminary Annual Report, 1971, Statistics
            Canada Cat. No. 84-201.

the very real economic gains achieved since Confederation. Between 1949
and 1967, Newfoundland's total personal income increased at an annual
average of 8.5 percent, the highest in Canada. But because of the acute
population increase, these gains were dissipated across a larger population. Thus the per capita income increased by only 6.5 percent annually
(*Newfoundland Bulletin,* December, 1968).

It should be noted that the effects of Newfoundland's high birth rate
on her economic development is by no means temporary. Even if the
birth rate immediately declined it would take twenty years for the large
juvenile population already born to reach the labour force. In the next
twenty years Newfoundland will have many more people entering the
labour force than leaving it through retirement and death. Although the

exact numbers are difficult to calculate, the Newfoundland government has estimated that it will have to produce 3,000 to 4,000 new jobs a year to absorb these additional workers, and its estimates are probably conservative (Newfoundland, 1970a:ii). This means that in addition to the jobs needed for the thousands presently unemployed, or employed only on a seasonal basis, upwards of 80,000 new jobs must be found over the next twenty years if many Newfoundlanders are not to be unemployed or forced to migrate. Obviously this is an enormous demand for a province where the labour force is now only about 160,000 persons.

Although it is fairly obvious that this rapid rate of population growth has had a detrimental effect on the economic well-being of Newfoundland in the past, and is likely to retard her economic growth for years to come, the Newfoundland government has made no effort to impede it. In fact it has revelled in the high birth rate. Politicians have argued repeatedly that a much larger populace is prerequisite to economic self-sufficiency, for it can then "support dozens of factories and other kinds of enterprise that couldn't survive today" (Smallwood, 1973:352). But while twice as many people would require approximately twice the present amount of goods and services, large industries tend to be more efficient than small ones and existing industries are likely to be able to double their capacity without doubling their labour force. Many new industries would have to be attracted to maintain even the current chronically bad employment-unemployment ratio.

Newfoundland's rate of population growth is only part of her population problem. Although more than 57 percent of the population now live in centres of 1,000 or more people (see Table 3), Newfoundland's rural population has continued to grow and has remained widely dispersed. As late as 1961, Newfoundland had 1,104 communities of which 815 had less than 300 inhabitants (see Table 4). While various community resettlement programmes succeeded in reducing these numbers so that by 1971 there were only 878 separate communities, there were still 545 with fewer than 300 residents and 226 with fewer than 100 occupants. Their small size and isolation make it extremely difficult to provide modern services for their inhabitants.

While the Newfoundland government has done little to curb population growth, it has been actively concerned about population dispersion. The resettlement policy is a direct response to this problem. From the point of view of the planners, Newfoundland's future primarily depends on the further development of seventy-seven selected growth centres.

Table 3

Percentages of Rural and Urban Population in Newfoundland for Census Years 1901 to 1971

Census Year	Total Census Population	Rural Population (under 1,000)	Per cent Rural	Urban Population (over 1,000)	Per cent Urban
1901	220,984	186,458	77.5	49,616	22.5
1911	242,619	186,485	76.9	56,161	23.1
1921	263,033	198,555	75.5	64,478	24.5
1935	289,588	203,986	70.4	85,602	32.0
1945	321,819	218,886	68.0	102,933	32.0
1951	361,416	206,621	57.2	154,795	42.8
1961	457,853	225,833	49.3	232,020	50.7
1966	493,396	226,707	45.9	266,689	54.1
1971	522,104	223,304	42.8	298,800	57.2

Sources: For 1901 to 1945: Compiled from statistics on communities of over 1,000 population given in *Census of Newfoundland,* 1945:2. For 1951 to 1966: Compiled from *Canada Year Book,* 1956, 1968. For 1971: Statistics provided by Statistics Canada. Urban and rural percentages calculated by the author.

As we shall see throughout this book, many rural Newfoundlanders regard this "solution" as a major attack on their goals and values and a threat to their way of life.

The fact that Newfoundland is an island presents a further obstacle to social and economic development. Goods produced in Newfoundland cannot be transported overland to markets, and the additional labour costs involved in loading goods from boats to trains or trucks places Newfoundland products at a disadvantage when competing with neighbouring provinces for North American markets. Isolation hampers Newfoundland's economic prospects in other ways as well. Although central Canadians tend to think of the Atlantic region as relatively small, St. John's is approximately the same distance by sea from Halifax as Halifax is from Boston. Thus goods produced in Newfoundland not only have to be loaded and unloaded several times, but they must also travel great

Table 4

Number of Communities in Newfoundland by Population in Census Years, 1961, 1966 and 1971

Population of Community		Number of Communities		
		1961	1966	1971
0 –	49	238	153	113
50 –	99	174	148	113
100 –	199	263	222	196
200 –	299	140	125	123
300 –	399	83	91	82
400 –	499	69	48	44
500 –	599	24	39	43
600 –	699	31	27	29
700 –	799	16	24	25
800 –	899	4	14	12
900 –	999	8	12	17
1,000 –	1,099	6	8	7
1,100 –	1,199	9	7	8
1,200 –	1,299	4	4	7
1,300 –	1,399	4	4	1
1,400 –	1,499	3	4	6
1,500 –	1,599	3	2	4
1,600 –	1,699	3	2	2
1,700 –	1,799	0	3	3
1,800 –	1,899	1	4	1
1,900 –	1,999	0	0	3
2,000 –	2,499	3	9	13
2,500 –	2,999	4	4	4
3,000 –	3,999	3	2	5
4,000 –	4,999	4	7	7
5,000 –	5,999	2	3	2
6,000 –	6,999	2	1	1
7,000 –	7,999	1	3	5
8,000 –	8,999	0	0	0
9,000 –	9,999	0	0	0

Table 4 (Continued)

Population of Community	Number of Communities		
	1961	1966	1971
10,000 – 19,999	0	0	0
20,000 – 29,999	1	1	1
30,000 and over	1	1	1
Total number of Communities	1,104	972	878

Sources: 1961: *Census of Canada* 1961, pp. 92-538, Bulletin SP—4 "Population of Unincorporated Places of 50 persons and over". *Canada Year Book,* 1968, p. 197, "Incorporated Towns and Villages, 1961"; and a supplement provided by Dominion Bureau of Statistics, St. John's, Newfoundland, listing "Unincorporated places with less than 50 persons".

Sources 1966 & 1971:   Lists provided by Statistics Canada in St. John's, Newfoundland showing "Province of New-foundland: Unincorporated Communities with a Population of less than 50 for 1966 and 1971"; "Population of Unincorporated Places of 50 Persons and Over, Newfoundland 1966 and 1971"; "Province of Newfoundland: Population of Incorporated Cities, Towns and Villages, Census Years 1951-1971".

The count of communities was made by the author from these census lists.

distances to reach their markets. This is clearly revealed in one of the favourite advertisements of Newfoundland's Department of Economic Development which shows a map of the world with Newfoundland at the centre and concentric circles drawn at 500-mile intervals around it. The accompanying text contends that Newfoundland is "right in the middle of everything", and goes on to explain that New York and central Canada are only 1,000 miles away to the east and London is but 2,000 miles to the west. The advertisement obviously wishes to convey an image of "the world centered on Newfoundland", but it suggests instead that Newfoundland is the one place in the western world which is farthest from *all* major world markets.

Problems within Newfoundland's labour force present another hindrance to social and economic development. Although major gains have been made in educating and training the labour force, a large segment remains illiterate. In 1961, 18 percent of all Newfoundlanders and 26.7 percent of Newfoundland's rural population were illiterate, giving Newfoundland twice the national illiteracy rate. The cost of training these workers to perform the highly technical work demanded by many modern industries is often prohibitive.

An examination of the structure of Newfoundland's labour force gives further insight into her economic problems (see Table 5). At the turn of the century nearly the entire labour force was made up of inshore fishermen. Although the popular image of Newfoundlanders as fishermen, loggers and miners still exists, these primary producers together now make up less than one-quarter of the labour force. In reality most Newfoundland workers are employed in the secondary and tertiary sectors of the economy.

While it is common in advanced societies to have a large segment of the labour force engaged in service (tertiary) activities, it is unusual in a society with such a small manufacturing base. In a sense Newfoundland has reached a "post industrial" stage of development without ever having established an industrial component in its economy. It can only maintain this because it is a part of the larger Canadian economy and can depend on Canadian transfer payments.

The relatively rapid shift from a traditional rural fishing economy to a modern, urban, commercial one has given Newfoundland some of the characteristics of a "dual economy". In a dual economy the traditional and modern sectors are "worlds apart" and operate relatively independently of one another. Often there is a major difference between the two sectors in their attitudes and values toward living and conducting business.[2] Although there is a danger of overemphasizing this dualism, it has important development implications. Policies which focus on urban development and assume that the traditional rural sector of the society will automatically adjust, may

---

[2]It is important to realize that a society with a rural-urban division does not *necessarily* have a dual economy. A dual economy implies that the traditional and modern segments operate virtually independently and that there are basic differences in the values of and the benefits derived by each segment.

only increase the schism. Development planning must include rural development plans which are based on the natural skills, crafts and resources of the
traditional economy, not simply extensions of urban policies into rural
areas. Plans should not be aimed at annihilating the traditional sector, but
at incorporating it into the overall economy.

Rapid population growth and dispersal, insularity, isolation, illiteracy
and a low level of industrial skills were all problems which faced Newfoundland at Confederation. They can be regarded as background conditions
which any social and economic development policy has had to try to overcome or alter. But the problems of economic dualism, small manufacturing
base, unbalanced labour force and dependence on federal transfer payments seem to be of a different order. Although they are partly the result
of insularity, isolation and illiteracy, they are also the product of the government's handling of these problems over the past twenty-five years
(Matthews, 1975a).

The Fate of the Outport Newfoundlander

These social and economic problems have severely tested the endurance of
many Newfoundlanders. In spite of the government's announcements of
proposed new industries and the opening of major developments like the
Churchill Falls power development or the Come-By-Chance oil refinery, the
province still does not have enough jobs for its population. Moreover, the
fishery which used to absorb much of the excess labour force is now in
competition with international fishing fleets and is unable to expand any
further.

Faced with these dismal employment prospects many Newfoundlanders
have chosen to move. Although the population grew from 347,000 to
510,000 between 1949 and 1971, there would have been thousands
more Newfoundlanders if the emigration rate from the province had not
been higher than ever before. From the late 1950s to the present, Newfoundlanders have been leaving their native land at an even greater rate
than during the hungriest period of the great Depression (see Table 6).

Yet in 1971 a greater number of Newfoundlanders (223,304) than ever
before lived in rural areas (Table 3). Some of these people still manage to
eke a living from the traditional sector of the economy. But most have
found it necessary to move back and forth between the two sectors, earning
only enough money from occasional wage employment to maintain the
important vestiges of their traditional life. These people are not part of the

Table 5

Employment in Newfoundland by Selected Industry, 1970 (Yearly Averages)

Industry	Number Employed
Primary:	
Forestry	2,200
Mining	5,900
Fishing	17,765*
(Fishing full time)	(8,855)
(Fishing part time)	(7,282)
(Fishing occasional)	(8,628)
Secondary:	
Manufacturing	12,600
(Non-durables)	(10,700)
(Durables)	(1,900)
Construction	7,600
Tertiary:	
Trade	18,200
(Wholesale)	(6,100)
(Retail)	(12,100)
Finance	2,300
Community, Business and Personal Services	30,300
(Non-commercial sector)	(21,600)
(Commercial sector)	(8,700)
Public Administration and Defence	8,600
Transportation, Communication and Other Utilities	14,600

*As the Newfoundland fishery is seasonal, many Newfoundland inshore fishermen are listed as part time and occasional even though they would regard themselves as full-time fishermen. However, a small number of them may also be employed in other industries (notably forestry) during the off season.

Source: Most of the data above are taken from "Estimates of Employees By Province and Industry", February 1971, Statistics Canada, Catalogue No. 72-008. This tabulation does not include fishermen. The data on fishing were taken from "Fisheries Statistics, Newfoundland 1971", Statistics Canada, Catalogue No. 24-202.

Table 6

Newfoundland: Average Yearly Net Migration and Net Migration per 1,000 Population, 1922-1971

Census Period	Total Natural Increase	Actual Population Gain	Total Net Migration*	Average Yearly Net Migration	Average Yearly Net Migration per 1,000 Population**
1922-35	43,416	26,555	−16,861	−1,204	−4.4
1936-45	47,837	32,231	−15,606	−1,561	−5.1
1946-51	54,596	39,579	−15,017	−2,503	−7.3
1952-56	53,623	53,658	+35	+7	0.0
1957-61	60,168	42,779	−17,389	−3,478	−8.2
1962-66	58,265	35,543	−22,722	−4,544	−9.5
1967-71	48,540	28,708	−19,832	−3,966	−7.5

*Minus figures indicate that the net migration was an out-migration. The actual figures indicate how many more people left the province than entered it.

**Rates of net migration were calculated on the average population during the census period. This was obtained by averaging the total population at the beginning and end of the census period.

urban society for, as is characteristic of a dual economy, their basic values and attitudes are those associated with rural life. Failure for them would mean moving their families to live permanently in Toronto, St. John's or Corner Brook.[3] Success, on the other hand, has come to be associated with the ability to supplement traditional sources of income with outside seasonal employment, so that one's family can live in their rural community throughout the year. These are the people of Small Harbour, Mountain Cove, and Grande Terre.

[3]This point has been missed repeatedly in studies of Atlantic province immigrants in Ontario. Most have described those who leave and return home as failures who were unable to survive in a more complex society. However from the point of view of the immigrants themselves, those who are able to return are often regarded as successes, particularly if they return after only a few years. For a study which does make this point clear see Anne E. Martin, *Up-along: Newfoundland Families in Hamilton.*

CHAPTER III

SMALL HARBOUR

The people of two communities in Notre Dame Bay have said point-blank that they will stay where they are. The following is a text of a telegram sent to the minister responsible for the resettlement programme, William Rowe, and the MHA for Green Bay, William Smallwood, and we quote that telegram:

> The people of Ship Harbour and Small Harbour are shocked over the recent statement by Member of Parliament, John Lundrigan. It is hard to believe that our government could have so little regard for human beings and reach such a deplorable decision. This decision by our government to strip us of our birthright and deny us of our freedom of choice is only the same as the Russians did in Czechoslovakia in 1968. Since 98 percent of the people of our community are opposed to the centralization programme we are proud to announce that we are here to stay. Therefore it is time for the government to abandon their attempt to force the people to move by denying them public services, and make a speedy decision to give our community the public services we are requesting but have long been denied.

M.P. John Lundrigan said last week that people in these communities were being forced to move by denial of services because the communities were on an official government list of communities slated for centralization. The telegram was signed by the secretary of the community council, on behalf of the people of Small Harbour and Ship Harbour.

News Item,
CJON Radio Network, May 12, 1969

"We are proud to announce that we are here to stay"[1]

In many ways the statement quoted above inaugurated this study. On May 12, 1969 I was driving across Newfoundland after spending three days with a rural development field worker. I had been totally involved in the problems of small rural communities as they attempted to organize

---

[1] I am greatly indebted to Robert Chanteloup for his insightful comments on a previous draft of this chapter. Dr. Chanteloup lived in Small Harbour for several months as part of his study of religious conversion in rural Newfoundland.

regional development councils. Almost everyone we talked with seemed convinced that such organizations were essential if communities like theirs were ever to develop. Yet it was readily apparent that inter-community co-operation was not easy to achieve and that organizational skills were sadly lacking. Most of the communities I visited would be easy prey for those wishing resettlement rather than redevelopment.

As I turned these experiences over in my mind, the car radio carried the news that two small communities on an isolated island 200 miles away had, through a community council acting on their behalf, declared that they would not be moved. To my knowledge they were (and still are) the only communities in Newfoundland to issue a statement publicly opposing the resettlement programme. Clearly they were unique, and I resolved to find out why. In August, 1970 I took a coastal boat to Small Harbour.

Small Harbour lies on the southwest shore of Centre Island, a nine-by-four-mile promontory off Newfoundland's northeast coast. Its 192 residents share this island with the 350 inhabitants of Ship Harbour, a community located almost directly across the island along the shores of Pleasant Arm. The island itself is at the outer edge of a small archipelago which stretches some twenty miles into the centre of Notre Dame Bay.

Small Harbour's recorded history is limited to sporadic census records and the inscriptions on tombstones in her graveyards.[2] The first permanent resident is not known, but there are local legends of pirates. Neither of the existing communities appears in Newfoundland's first census of 1836, although there is some evidence that permanent settlement began at this time.[3] By 1857 there were definitely 150 persons living on the island, and the census of 1874 shows Small Harbour and Pleasant Arm having a combined population of 110, with two other communities on the island having a total of 155 persons. Small Harbour first appears alone in the census of 1884 when it had only 59 residents. The population had risen to 114 by the turn of the century (1901), stood at 223 in 1935, and peaked in the 1950s before falling to 231 in 1966 and to 192 in 1971.

---

[2] I am indebted to a former resident who wrote a history of Small Harbour in 1969 as a project for a course in Newfoundland history at Memorial University of Newfoundland. Several residents of Small Harbour proudly displayed copies of this paper. The paper is an analysis of census records combined with anecdotal information collected from some of the island's residents.

[3] A listing under another name in that year may refer to Centre Island.

The original settlers were undoubtedly part of a slow dispersion of population from the main centres of Twillingate and Fogo, approximately 100 miles to the east.[4] These large communities were early fishing centres where British-based mercantile houses carried on an active trade with locally-based fishermen. As the fishing grounds became overcrowded, the more adventurous fishermen simply rowed their small dories westward in search of more bountiful locations. Centre Island seemed an obvious place to settle. Located well out in the bay, it had the advantage of being near the major fishing banks, and had numerous sheltered harbours, a plentiful supply of wood, water and small game, and relatively arable land.

The early settlers lacked many facilities—a situation they must have pondered during their long row to Twillingate for their annual supplies. Without faith in Divine Providence their position might often have seemed hopeless. As early as 1857 they erected a Church of England on the island but were only able to observe sacraments such as baptism and communion during the rare and sporadic visits of an ordained priest. A second denomination, Wesleyan Methodism, soon gained popularity because it gave its adherents the attention they lacked. Half the population of Centre Island had been converted to Methodism by 1869, and by 1884 Small Harbour had its own Wesleyan church. Yet even Wesleyism could not afford the luxury of a resident clergyman to perform sacraments on a regular basis, and it too gave place to a denomination willing to provide even more services for the people. The Salvation Army required less training for its clergy before ordination and accepted both men and women as its officers. It was able to provide spiritual leaders to many small communities needing pastors rather than theologians. The census of 1901 lists four Salvation Army adherents on the island, but by 1921 there were 123, and a new church had been built at Small Harbour where most of their members resided. In the years which followed the United (Wesleyan) Church remained relatively strong in the Pleasant Arm area (now renamed Ship Harbour) while approximately two-thirds of the population of Small Harbour transferred their allegiance to "the Army".

Formal education was less important than religion to the settlers of Centre Island. Children learned the skills of fishing and housekeeping

---

[4]This is suggested by the high proportion of native-born Newfoundlanders among the population. The listing for Pleasant Arm in 1857 appears to include all residents of the island and shows that 147 out of 150 were born in Newfoundland. In 1874 the combined population of the island was 265, of whom 261 were native sons.

from their parents, since no school was built until 1889. This one-room structure at Small Harbour was quickly follwed by a second on the other side of the island. In Newfoundland the educational system has always been divided along religious lines, and even today several separate school boards represent each of the major religious denominations. Each denomination has its own schools in every community where it is represented. As a result there is a proliferation of one-room schools, each manned by a minimally trained teacher who strives to provide meaningful education to all levels simultaneously. As the Centre Islanders had a propensity towards religious conversion, they soon had a number of one-room schools. By the late 1960s there were seven separate schools on the island, only one of which had two classrooms.

Fish and potatoes have always been the basis of the Centre Island economy. In the early years there were enough cod on the nearby shoals for all. But as population grew, fishermen from all along Newfoundland's northeast coast were forced to travel north along the "French Shore" and to the Labrador coast in order to obtain enough fish. Increased fish prices made this a profitable venture, and soon most of Newfoundland's hamlets had their own fleet of sailing ships. By 1911 there were at least fifteen locally based vessels on Centre Island. These employed many local men and upwards of a hundred men from other communities. During the summer months Small Harbour was alive with ships putting in to take on water, or seeking shelter from a sudden squall. As soon as fishing ended in the fall, many of these ships set sail for St. John's, Halifax, Boston and beyond to pick up winter supplies and the next season's fishing gear. In these ports crew members would "sign on" as deckhands on larger vessels and spend part of their winter sailing to the Mediterranean for salt or to the West Indies with dried cod. In that pre-automobile age the men of Small Harbour were among the most mobile in the world.

The Depression of the 1930s destroyed the market for cod and Newfoundland's economy as well. Almost overnight the vessels disappeared and rural communities began their long decline. Even confederation with Canada did little to make them economically viable again.

Small Harbour in 1971 was a community bustling with activity. No sooner had our ship entered the harbour than one could hear the raucous staccato of chain saws over the continuous grind of heavy tractors. Workmen were building a road from Small Harbour to Ship Harbour, and were upgrading the village paths to the point where they could take motor vehicles. There were signs of other recent changes. A throbbing diesel generating station, located in a large, galvanized metal building in the heart of the community, now provided electricity to homes all over the island.

The credit for these accomplishments was directly linked, at least in the minds of community respondents, to their "proclamation" of 1969, and to the formation in November, 1967, of the combined community council representing all island communities. Why Small Harbour and her sister community came to form a community council is not completely clear. One community leader suggested that it was formed largely out of frustration with government inaction.

> It was here in Small Harbour and in Ship Harbour as well. We get together and have a chat, you know, and talk about what you think should be done and how it should be done. We tried on different occasions to get lights; we tried on different occasions to get a road; but we didn't seem to be heard owing to we had no local government or anything.

Little seems to have happened for fifteen months after the community council was formed. Then a Small Harbour representative resigned and was replaced by the main shopkeeper in Small Harbour in a subsequent by-election. He was not its formal leader, but his presence seems to have spurred the council to action.

> So we started right off the bat then. It's been eighteen months now and you can see what we've accomplished. We got $200,000 worth of electricity last year, and we got a beginning on the road. We're guaranteed a $24,000 post office this fall, and we're guaranteed the telephones this fall. I'll say we've accomplished more in fifteen months than any other council that ever was founded.

These accomplishments may not have been solely the result of action by the community council, but the result of a major tactical error by the federal government.

In the course of their efforts the community council petitioned the federal government for a new central post office to serve both island communities. In his reply the minister responsible apparently indicated that he could not seriously consider their request because both Small Harbour and Ship Harbour were on a provincial government list of communities which were to be resettled. The provincial government had long maintained that there was no list of communities "slated for resettlement", and had argued that the decision to resettle was always a local decision. The federal disclosure therefore caused them considerable embarrassment and it was quickly turned into a *cause célèbre* with far-reaching repercussions.

In some way the news director of CJON radio and television learned of the affair. Just how this happened is unclear, but he may well have been contacted by members of Small Harbour's community council. In any case he sent a telegram to the main shopkeeper in Small Harbour (who was now also the key figure in council affairs), asking him for his views on the subject. In co-operation with some other council members, the shopkeeper immediately drafted the proclamation of protest which was heard on radio throughout Newfoundland. Although the statement was purportedly issued by the community council on behalf of the people, most residents learned of it only after it was made public. Those who were instrumental in drafting it justified their action by claiming that they had "been dealing with the people long enough to know what their wishes were".

The (Progressive Conservative) member of parliament for the area immediately demanded that the (Liberal) provincial and federal governments "prove" that Centre Island was not about to be resettled.

> So this is where the dirt was stirred up. . . . John Lundrigan, he got on our side. He told the provincial government, "If it's not true . . . get out and prove it then. Give them the lights."

Holding this political firecracker, both governments rushed to shower Centre Island with amenities. Lights, a road and even the promise of a new post office were thrust upon them. It is no wonder that members of the community council used hyperbole in describing their accomplishments, even though some of their good fortune may have resulted from circumstances over which they had little influence. Indeed, the role of the community council in the whole affair is shrouded in mystery. They seem to have accomplished little until the traditional merchant-leader joined them. With his involvement the council suddenly took on new life and petitioned all levels of government for improved services.

The actual process by which Small Harbour obtained improvements has implications for our study. I originally became interested in Small Harbour because it and Ship Harbour were the only communities in all of Newfoundland which had both formed a community council and rejected the pressures to resettle. This seemed to suggest that some form of intercommunity co-operation and formal organization operated in the community, enabling the residents to make and carry out decisions which would affect their future. But most people had no prior knowledge of their public proclamation. This supposedly collective sentiment had actually been drafted by a few community leaders. There was also little to suggest that any strong spirit of community co-operation had ever existed. Historically the community had been divided by religious cleavages as the numerous churches and one-room schools bore witness. Although the formation of a community council seemed to indicate a new spirit of co-operation, a closer look at its origins and mode of operation revealed the existence of an elite organization, rather than a wide base of social co-operation.

What were the true "wishes of the majority of the people"? Were most residents of Small Harbour really "proud to announce that they were there to stay", or was this the decision which the traditional leaders hoped that they would make? Moreover, did the provision of services really ensure that they would stay? To answer these questions we must examine more closely the pattern of life in Small Harbour and the attitudes and values of the residents.

"There's a lot of people went out of it"

Is Small Harbour a community in decline? A major indicator of community decline is population decline and, as we have already indicated, the population of Small Harbour has decreased some 18 percent from its peak during the early 1950s. The high rate of out-migration was obvious from our survey sample. From the post office list of forty household heads, thirty members of the general population and three merchants who appeared to be potential community leaders were selected. Although the list was only two years old, fully nineteen of the thirty-three householders were not in the community: nine had moved away (they had either taken their families with them, or were single men with little to tie them to the community); seven other men were away working, but had wives and families remaining in the community; one household head was away in hospital; two others had died. Those who had moved away had travelled to Labrador, Ontario or to nearby communities. Of the six families in nearby communities, four were in "mainland" communities with road access to the outside world, while two others had moved to a nearby island community which is, despite its isolation, a centre of economic activity within the region. The seven persons from our sample who were still residents of Small Harbour but who were away working, were employed either in some aspect of the fishery (e.g. fish inspector), as crew members of trading boats or as construction workers. This extensive out-migration meant that only fourteen formal interviews were completed.

Movement from Small Harbour is by no means a new phenomenon. Every household head whom we interviewed reported that he had a sibling living elsewhere.[5] In the traditional marriage pattern there is a greater tendency for women to move than men. Thus the husbands in our sample had a total of thirty-one sisters living in other communities and only ten still in Small Harbour. Brothers were evenly divided, with eleven living in Small Harbour and eleven living elsewhere. There is every sign that migration from the community is accelerating among the younger generation. The respondents had thirty children aged eighteen and over. Of these, only five lived in Small Harbour.[6] Ten of the respondents themselves had worked elsewhere for various periods of time. Most of these had been engaged as loggers or employed in the Labrador fishery. However only three of our respondents had worked away from the community in the preceding five years.

In sum, the community has seen at least two generations of accelerating out-migration. One-third of the present household heads work elsewhere, separated from their families for long periods of the year either because they are unable to afford the cost of relocating their family, or because they wish to remain in Small Harbour.

With the exception of two people over seventy-five years old, the sample was generally middle-aged, with an average (mean) age of 46.7 years. Although poorly educated by most standards, two of our sample had completed grade ten and another six had completed at least grade seven, which is somewhat higher than normal for that age group in most rural Newfoundland communities. Of the fourteen household heads interviewed, twelve were born in Small Harbour, while the remaining two were born less than five miles away. Eight of the twelve who were married had chosen wives from outside their birthplace, but all of the wives were Newfoundland-born.

Despite the long period of out-migration and the slow decline in population in recent years, one could argue that only the excess population has left. There are, for example, no abandoned homesites, and most resi-

[5] In all but one case these siblings previously had lived in Small Harbour.

[6] There were an additional forty-eight children under age eighteen, of whom thirty were less than ten years old. Only three of this total group were living outside the community; two as students and a third as a domestic servant.

dents do not consider Small Harbour a declining community. Few are even aware of the extent of emigration. Most estimated that only three or four families had left in the preceding five years.

> There've been about three moved out. But then
> somebody got married and keeped the number up.

Only the aged appeared to reflect on the overall trend. One elderly gentleman rattled off a list of fifteen families who had moved, while another announced that "twenty-two families are moved out of this in my time". Both persons were referring to a period of seventy years.

Residents denied that out-migration had affected community life in any substantial way. Many indicated that those who left had been drains on the community and society, and implied that the place was better off without them.

> No. I wouldn't say it had. They were people living on social
> assistance or welfare. They're not turning in anything to the
> government. They're only an expense.
> Two of them was old age pensioners and I don't see where
> that would make much difference to the place.

Still others emphasized that accomplishments had been achieved without them:

> Well, we got the lights since the two of them went, and we
> got the road since they went.

The implication is that those who had moved had given up on the community prematurely.

Part of the reason for such low estimates of migration is that few *families* migrate. Most of those who move are young people who drift away to a variety of initially temporary, if ultimately permanent jobs and their departure is not as obvious as the premeditated move of a whole family. Even though most of the residents of Small Harbour spoke positively about the community, they encourage their own children to leave. Most felt that there was simply nothing on the island for young people to do.

> I don't think there's anything here on this island for them. They
> can't make a living here anyway.

Only three respondents disagreed. One offered insights into the dilemma facing young people:

> If they'd stay here they could make the community a better place,
> but I don't know if they could make a living here or not. Those

fellows going to university, it must be hard for them to settle down
here.

Only one man suggested an alternative means of livelihood for those who
might wish to remain.

> Well, if you got an education there's no way to use it here. . . . But
> there is ways that several more families could make a living on this
> island. Say there's room here for a farmer, maybe two. Then there's
> a poultry farm. There's a lot of chicken and eggs eat around this bay.
> And a sawmill. There's 20,000 cord of wood on this island.

Ironically, his own children had left the island years before.

It seems safe to conclude that the normal process whereby excess
population emigrates had become transformed, in the case of Small
Harbour, into a process of general community decline. Not only was
the community unable to provide sustaining employment for its existing
adult population, but it encouraged its children to move away. Nevertheless, at the time of the study, many residents were beginning to think that
the "tide had turned" and the community was beginning to develop again.

"She's just picking up again"

> We're just started here and we're fifteen years behind. It's only now
> two years since the council's been formed, and now we're getting
> ahead. We never had nothing before. . . . She was going down for eight
> years or so, and now she's just picking up again.

Such was the hopeful sentiment of most of the residents of Small
Harbour. After several decades of out-migration and decline, things did
indeed seem to be "picking up again". The road and electricity were seen
as the main indicators of a revival, but there were also other encouraging
changes. The most important of these in the minds of the community
members and in the effect it was having, was the appearance of a new
religious group in the community.

Religion had always been an important factor in the life of Small
Harbour, but, as we saw earlier, there had been great difficulties in
attracting a resident clergyman. Frustration led many community
members to abandon their traditional faith for another denomination
which could satisfy their spiritual and social needs more directly. The
Salvation Army, which proselytized the community between the 1920s
and the 1950s, gained the followers that other denominations lost.
Their church stands almost next door to that of the United Church,

but when this study was conducted, it had been months since a clergyman had preached in either church. Like the Church of England and the
United Church before them, the Salvationists found it almost impossible
to staff some of their churches. Their last resident officer in Small Harbour
was a single woman who left the community after only two months. Both
the Salvation Army and United Church buildings in Small Harbour remained locked, as abandoned and desolate as the nearby graveyards.

Across the harbour, however, hammers were at work putting the
finishing touches on a third church for the community: Small Harbour
was in the midst of a religious conversion. For nearly a year a Pentecostal
pastor had been stationed in the community. This man had grown up on
a nearby island, had been sent to Ontario for training and had served in
other parts of Newfoundland before arriving in Small Harbour. According to the pastor, the decision to station him in Small Harbour was made
after an expedition to the area by one of the church officials. According to the people, he had been sent to Small Harbour in response to a
petition from local residents. The man responsible for this petition provided this account:

> I went up to Robert's Arm on Sunday to see the pastor up there,
> and told him we wanted a pastor on Centre Island, wanted the
> gospel preached, I said. He said, "Why? Where's your Lieutenant
> to? What about the Salvation Army?" I said, "Sir, as far as I'm
> concerned the Army is gone to the wall. Down there all the day
> there's no Sunday school for the children." I said, "We wants a
> church there." "Well," he said, "if you can get eight names, we'll
> come in Small Harbour and build you a church!" So I got seven-
> teen names and carried them up to him. And after that they just
> started coming here.[7]

For the first few months the Pentecostal pastor held services in the
United Church building. After four months the United Church minister
of a neighbouring island, whose charge also included Small Harbour, came
at the request of some United Church members and "drove the pastor
out of the United Church". The Salvation Army pastor set about constructing his own church. His long hours of hard work, during which he
almost singlehandedly built both a church and a house for himself and
his wife, earned him the respect of most community members. His acceptance was eased even more because he was from salvationist stock

[7]This quote is taken from the field notes of Dr. Robert Chanteloup, who has kindly
consented to its use here.

and his services were generally familiar to local residents, and because his wife was a teacher who began to teach in one of the schools. The latter was important since there was considerable danger that some classrooms might be closed for lack of students. The presence of his wife ensured that there would be a teacher even if this should happen.

This does not mean that there was no opposition to his coming. The traditional community leaders were aligned with the older religious denominations and none was among the petitioners for the new church. As the new church began to dominate community affairs it threatened to upset the traditional class balance within the community. The tensions and conflicts which arose cut across traditionally harmonious relationships, even to the extent of splitting families.

Despite the tensions his arrival created the Pentecostal pastor had filled an important spiritual and social need during the year he had been in the community. Even if no Salvation Army or United Church clergy were available, there were still people to be married, children to be baptized and the dead to be buried. His Sunday services and twice-weekly prayer meetings had both a spiritual and a social function, providing a focus for the daily lives of many residents. It was just like the old days. For the first time in several years there was some place to go.

To some degree the community's acceptance of the Pentecostal pastor was facilitated by the actions of his United Church counterpart. Although local residents had asked the United Church minister to evict the Pentecostals from their place of worship, they disliked his method of accomplishing the task. His eviction visit had been his first in several months, and once he had performed this task, he did not reappear in the community for several more. Even his staunchest supporters could not forgive him for this neglect.

> He's supposed to come every second week. He's been here once since last September or October. That was when they sent for him and he drove the pastor out of the church.

Many even went so far as to suggest that his only interest was the money he collected from Small Harbour.

> When he gets down low in [the nearby community], he come over here. He only comes when the need arises.

The money collected from such a small community would cover only a small part of the pastor's salary and expenses, but this explanation was accepted by many residents and repeated frequently.

The United Church clergyman made one of his infrequent visits to
the community while we were there, arriving unexpectedly on a Sunday
afternoon. He may have intended to hold services but he was prevented
from doing so because the Small Harbour resident who held the keys
to the church had disappeared with them.

> Nobody didn't know he was coming. The man who've got the key
> didn't see him. How we do it, I take the key two or three weeks and
> pass it over to someone else and they take the key, and the man
> who had the key didn't know he was coming. . . . He [the key holder]
> was here yes, but there was no bell rang, and he [the clergyman] went
> on back to Ship Harbour.

As far as can be determined this was a deliberate strategy on the part of
some members of the United Church congregation to show the United
Church clergyman that they no longer depended on him, and to
communicate to the United Church that, unless it served them better, it
would lose them as adherents and as a source of money. Although this
strategy was appropriate from their standpoint, it likely had the effect
of further alienating the United Church clergyman from the community.

In sum, although some still deplored the new denomination because,

> They're just building up one church to let two others fall down.
> It's like a new style. People go to the new churches like they do
> new styles.

and because it undermined established authority patterns and created
new schisms, most members of the community were beginning to accept,
if not to welcome its presence. "We goes over to Pentecost now," said
one resident, "but we're still Salvation Army." Most forecast a strong
future for the new church despite the fact that there had been only five
converts to date.

> I think that church is going to take everybody. The other churches
> will go down and if we're going to church we got no choice. The
> [Salvation] Army can't get an officer. The people is too small now
> and they got no other choice. If people are going to church at all, we
> got to go there [the Pentecostal Church].
> The way it is, I don't think the Salvation Army is ever going to rise
> here again. People want somewhere for their children to go—Sunday
> school and so on. They [the Pentecostals] take the lead here now.

By the time we left the community, several residents had been converted
to the new faith, and the new church was rapidly becoming the centre of
social and spiritual life in the community.

"We're still in the dark ages as far as schools are concerned"

Most residents of Small Harbour were eager to claim that things in their community were "picking up". Certainly, if one were to go by the level of activity in the community, this seemed to be true. Yet in spite of their assertions that life in their community was changing for the better, one fundamental worry continued to bother them—the school system. Their concern originated with the provincial government's decision several years before to build a central high school to serve all the communities in the district. This was subsequently built in a community on the nearby mainland, some twenty miles by sea from Small Harbour.

For most communities in the region the school was a remarkable step forward. No longer must their children be satisfied with an inadequate high school education in a one-room school. They could be bussed daily to a modern school where they would be taught by well-qualified teachers. But for Small Harbour this new school created a major dilemma. Local children were unable to commute to school because the island community was cut off from the mainland by ice and high seas for much of the winter. Instead, when they reached the high school age of fourteen or fifteen, Small Harbour children had to leave home and live in boarding houses near the school. They were able to journey home for an occasional weekend during the autumn, but there were months on end during which they could not see their families.

Any parent might be unhappy with a situation in which his children were separated from their family at such an early age, but it was particularly distasteful to many Small Harbour parents. Formal education has not been highly valued in rural Newfoundland until very recently. Most children left school early and learned the skills of fishing and homemaking from their parents. In addition most Newfoundlanders maintain extensive kin ties and great emphasis is placed on family life. To have children carried away at such an early age not only placed massive strains on the children, but it also undermined their parents' conception of themselves and their worth.

There was also general dissatisfaction with the quality of education being meted out in the junior schools remaining in the community. Approximately two-thirds of our sample indicated that the "chances for [their] children to get an education in Small Harbour are poor". They felt that there were too many one-room schools and not enough teachers with university degrees. One community leader claimed:

> We're still in the dark ages as far as schools are concerned. On this island we got six one-room schools and one two-room school. . . . As the standard is, I thinks its bad. Though there's as many comes out of it [graduates] as anywhere else. When the grade nine to elevens go out they got to work desperately hard to catch up. The people feel that here it [educational standards] is below [that of other places]. Nobody is satisfied with the one-room schools. We're trying to work on a new school.

The problems of commuting and of poor primary education worried Small Harbour parents, but the most ominous threat of all was that declining school enrollment jeopardized existing facilities. The Newfoundland Department of Education regulations require that there be a minimum number of students per classroom. If numbers fall below a certain level, they simply eliminate the salary available for one of the teachers. In Small Harbour this would mean that they would eliminate a one-room school.

During the time we were in Small Harbour it became doubtful that there would be enough pupils to open one of the schools. Most residents considered this a major catastrophe. Ultimately the school was able to open, but as one school board member explained:

> If we'd have lost one more pupil this year, we'd have lost a room. So if one big family went, the schooling would get bad enough right there we'd have to move.

The response may seem overly dramatic until one realizes that the prime reason given for resettling was the desire for better schooling (Matthews, 1970). The continuing deterioration of school facilities on the island would prompt some residents to consider moving. "If we don't get a high school here," one said, "we'll all have to go." Two of the men who repeatedly expressed this sentiment have large families and the absence of one or both of these may result in closed classrooms. Thus the future of Small Harbour appears to be intimately tied to future developments in its educational facilities.

"We didn't know what to do, go or stay"

To most outsiders, life in an outport such as Small Harbour seems tranquil and unchanging. But to those who live there, every day brings new promises and hopes, despair and fears. In recent years roads, lights and

a new church have all come to Small Harbour; during that same time
people have left and the schools, in most people's eyes, have "gone down".
Such changes would affect any community, but in Small Harbour, where
people are aware that they live on the brink of abandonment as a community, even the smallest change may have major implications.

How then do the people of Small Harbour regard their community and
evaluate its future? Their proclamation indicated that they were deeply
committed to the community, but is this really the sentiment of the
majority of residents? Each of the families interviewed were asked
whether they thought life in Small Harbour had improved or declined
in the past fifteen or twenty years. Somewhat surprisingly given recent
developments, less than half of the respondents felt that their community
had improved. Those who did pointed to the new amenities. But the
majority of household heads felt that the community had declined because of extensive out-migration and the failing fishing economy.

> There's a lot of people went out of it. A lot of homes went out. A lot
> of merchants left. This was a flourishing community in the 1930s in
> regards of labour. A lot of merchants here owned their own vessels.
> I would say it has declined in the last fifteen years, and the reason for
> that is that the Premier said, "Haul up your boats and let them rot,
> there'll be two jobs for every man." People thought that was going
> to be a reality and it proved to be a fake. Everyone did away with
> their schooners. There used to be fifteen schooners here one time
> fishing, and 200 men going fishing, coming here and getting berths.

As the above quote indicates, there was a tendency to foreshorten history.
The prosperous fishery was destroyed by the Depression of the 1930s, and
most fishing schooners had disappeared long before the 1950s when
Premier Smallwood was reputed to have encouraged people to burn
their boats.

The attitude of Small Harbour residents toward their community became clearer when the subject of resettlement was raised. Although the
residents had heard of resettlement, all denied that they intended to move.
This is a common pattern: many people deny any desire to leave right
up to the moment of doing so. They could hardly do otherwise
without being branded as traitors, for their departure makes life
harder for those who remain and likely hastens the day when they, too,
might be forced out. But in Small Harbour half of the respondents, including all those who might be considered community leaders, were
willing to admit that they had considered moving at one time. Their com-

ments revealed a wide range of reasons for *not* going.

> We've talked about it, but I don't know where to go to better
> myself. I can't do nothing beside fish.

> Well I did a few years ago, yes. . . . I had a small business and I was
> getting tired of it after twenty years.

> If I could get a job. . . .

> We thought we might better ourself. We didn't know what to do;
> go or stay. So I decided I'd stay.

If resettlement had provided an attractive alternative, the residents would
have moved. However most Small Harbour men have been to the nearby
relocation centres and many have even worked there. In their opinion
these centres offer no possibility of lasting employment. They have
chosen not to move simply because resettlement does not hold out a
better alternative. From their perspective, it would *not* be a sensible
decision.

This became quite clear when they were asked to compare their way
of life with that of nearby communities, specifically, Robert's Arm and
Springdale. Both are likely "reception centres" and some former residents
of Small Harbour already live in them. Robert's Arm is a small village
like Small Harbour, but it is located on the mainland and linked to the
rest of the province by road. Its primary disadvantage is that it is too far
up the bay to sustain a viable fishery. Springdale is a regional supply
centre of approximately 3,000 people located on the mainland some
twenty miles from Small Harbour.

No one spoke favourably of Robert's Arm: Small Harbour people
thought it was a more expensive place in which to live, and that the employment prospects were scarce. We received several gloomy pictures of
people struggling to find work or languishing on welfare.

> It's cheaper to live here. If I go into Robert's Arm to live, I got a lot
> of things to pay.

> If I go to Robert's Arm, I'd starve to death—I think I would. Most
> of them may have a job, but for me to go there would be the
> finish.

> You don't see so many lying along the government wharf here as
> you do in Robert's Arm or Springdale. You can go up there when
> you like and the wharf is lined with people with nothing to do,
> only lie around. You don't see nothing like that here. Only a few
> youngsters out there swimming. Everybody's occupied at something
> here.

Springdale also offered little attraction. Although two people did mention that it was cheaper to buy food in the supermarkets there, and another three indicated that school and hospital facilities were better, others felt that there would be no permanent jobs for them there.

In fact, most respondents ignored both communities when they attempted to explain their decision to remain in Small Harbour. Most emphasized that it was cheaper for them to live on the island than anywhere else because they owned their own houses and had few other expenses. Others noted that it was possible to fish from Small Harbour, that they were self-sufficient, and that the people just seemed "more contented" there.

Given these attitudes, it is not surprising that resettlement officials have had little success in getting people to move, even though reportedly they have visited the community at least twice. One community leader gave us this account of a reported visit by the director of resettlement himself:

> He was set down there talking to me and he said, "What's your opinion?" And I told him. And he said, "We got three or four requests from Small Harbour." And I said, "Name them." He named them out and I said, "That's an old-aged pensioner and a fellow on social welfare." "Damm it," he said, "we don't care about those people. The people we move, we want them to go to work." That was the answer he gave to me. So he said, "If there's no more interest than that here, then I'll go again." So he went on and he's never been back since. . . . That was seven years ago, first when it came up. But I thinks there were two fellows touched in here one time since that from their office in Grand Falls.

However another resident seems to have been more intimidated by one of these visits.

> Q. Did anyone come to you?
> A. Oh yes. They were talking about it, and I said, "Go to somebody else."
> Q. Who came to you?
> A. I don't know. It was a stranger. I didn't ask him.
> Q. Someone from outside the place came?
> A. Yes. I said, "Go to somebody else." This is my home and if the other fellows stay here. I'm going to stay. But if all the other fellows goes out of it well, I'll have to follow, too.

His comments were part of the community's general condemnation of resettlement. Most could see little point in moving elsewhere if there was no work. One person on welfare even conceded, "It's just as well for the government to feed me here as in Robert's Arm." A storekeeper and an active fisherman in the community argued that resettlement might be right for some places, but not for Small Harbour. In the words of the latter:

> There's no place where the people here could get a better living. A lot of these people are in their fifties and sixties, and they'd all end up living on the government.

Although two people did indicate that resettlement was a good idea "because the government should be saving the money they're spending in a place like this", our sample unanimously agreed that the whole community was against it. There had been considerable talk of resettlement in the past, but the provision of electricity and roads reduced, at least temporarily, the more extreme dissatisfaction. As proof of the extent of their resolve to remain we were given this pithy insight:

> The way it is here, they're now putting concrete pillars under their houses. They're going to stay here until they got no other remedy.

Most of those with whom we talked seemed content to remain as long as the schools and transportation improved. We were told frequently that the island needed a causeway linking it to the mainland. The more realistic admitted that they would settle for a regular ferry service and in fact this service was provided some six months later. It operates daily throughout the nine months of the year that the bay is free of ice and travels to several of the nearby islands, linking them to one another as well as to the nearby mainland. When regular ferry service was established, the isolation of Centre Island was greatly reduced. Since it allowed children to return home from school on weekends, it also helped to alleviate the problem of family breakups.

But even though this service cuts some of the isolation and privation, Small Harbour still has one major problem: there is nothing for local residents to do. When questioned about this, most of our respondents suggested many ways of giving the island an economic base. Some elderly men, recalling the old days, felt that the government should provide for a new schooner fishery; middle-aged men argued for assistance to build longliners; others proposed saw mills, logging operations, chicken ranches and farms.

All of these suggestions came in reply to our question concerning how the government might assist people to earn a better living. When we asked how the people might better themselves, our queries were met with stony silence. A few vaguely recognized the need to "pull together", because "there's not five people on the island got the one mind". But only two respondents were able to propose anything that local residents could initiate without government assistance. Both were on the community council and were community leaders. One suggested that, if they could form a producers' co-operative, it might be possible to obtain loans for economic development that are not available to individual residents. But he saw lack of management experience as a major obstacle to success. The other leader listed a number of possible fishing and farming ventures and indicated that all had been discussed by the council, but could not suggest any way of starting them. As he explained:

> The council is trying. But the council don't want to go into business. We'd like it if it could be started under the name of some corporation, you know.

Lack of imagination, lack of organizational skill, lack of capital, lack of markets and isolation are still obstacles to the economic development of Small Harbour. Until these difficulties are overcome and new jobs are created, the people of Small Harbour will have to leave to find work. Many who do will not come back.

Commentary

One hundred years ago Small Harbour was an isolated outpost: travel was primarily by rowboat, and the nearest major centre was several days journey away. Life was harsh. Fifty years ago Small Harbour was a minor commercial centre for the Labrador fishing industry, and hundreds of men and ships came to her harbour every year. This was her heyday. But life was still a struggle: there was no electricity and little creature comfort. Today every house in Small Harbour has electricity and there are roads and a new ferry. Television, radio and the community's radio telephone provide communication with the outside world. In time of emergency help is usually available in minutes by sea-plane or helicopter. The days of discomfort and isolation are over and, in this respect, the people of Small Harbour have never had it so good.

Yet Small Harbour today may be on the verge of extinction. There is little for her people to do either for employment or amusement. While radio and television provide some entertainment, they also tell of opportunities for work and personal development elsewhere. Under such circumstances it is likely that the young will continue to leave Small Harbour and the population will continue to decline. At the very time when life in Small Harbour can at last be said to have a modicum of comfort and ease, many of her residents are tempted to abandon the community. Such is the irony of modernization.

Small Harbour is almost totally dependent on the outside world for survival and has very little control over its own fate. The extent of this dependency can be seen in the community's efforts to obtain modern facilities. It is unlikely that the community council would have been effective in getting facilities had it not been for the bureaucratic bumbling of government officials. The community's lack of control over its own fate is also obvious in the sphere of religion. Small Harbour has been unable to attract a resident clergyman for any of its traditional churches. Although some residents were apparently instrumental in attracting a new religious group to the community, there is no guarantee that the new church will survive. Other churches to which the residents have given their allegiance and their souls in the past have been forced to close their doors. Thus the real situation of the community contrasts vividly with the romanticized picture of the small rural community as the one remaining self-sufficient entity in this fragmented, urbanized society.

The people of Small Harbour are in a double bind. They are at the mercy of outside bureaucrats on one hand and at the mercy of their own neighbours on the other. Should one or more large families leave, schoolrooms will be closed and other families will feel compelled to leave. One community leader, who does manage to obtain an adequate living on the island, dubbed this process "the tyranny of the weak". It is but another aspect of the dependence of the people of Small Harbour.

Small Harbour has been left behind in the process of modernization. But, while it is largely the *victim of modernization,* it continues to exist only because it has become the *client of modernization.* My argument here is a modification of Alvin Gouldner's analysis of the role of the welfare state in his book, *The Coming Crisis in Western Sociology* (1970).

Gouldner contends that the modern developed state is a welfare state which values people primarily in terms of their utility (pp. 61-76). But in the modern welfare state many people are rendered "useless" to society by the process of modernization. A central problem for the modern welfare state is, therefore, the treatment of these "useless" people. As Gouldner elaborates:

A central problem confronting a society organized around utilitarian

values is the disposal and control of useless men. They may, for example, be sociologically separated and isolated in spatially distinct
locales where they are not painfully visable to the "useful"! They
may be placed, as American Indians were, on reservations; they
may come to live in ethnic ghettos, as American Blacks do; if they
have the means to do so, they may elect to live in benign environ-
ments such as the communities for the aged in Florida; they may be
placed in special training or retraining camps as are certain unskilled
and unemployed American youth, frequently Black; or again, they
may be placed in prisons or in insane asylums, following routine
certification by judicial or medical authorities.

Transition to a Welfare State does not simply mean transition from
a standard of individual to collective utility; it also implies a greater
involvement of the state in developing and managing the disposal
of the "useless" (pp. 76-77).

I would argue that rural people, particularly those living in a traditional
environment like that of Small Harbour, are regarded as peripheral and
essentially "useless" by the planners of modernization. Some planners
freely admitted that resettlement was likely to be to the detriment of
many adults, but that it would ultimately be of benefit to their children.
Even many of those who agreed to be resettled did so with full knowledge that there was little employment for them in their chosen growth
centre. They, too, had come to regard themselves as "useless", and had
moved so that their children might have a future in an urbanized society.

But as Gouldner observes, the modern nation state is a welfare state.
It does not simply define people as useless. It is committed to the process of rehabilitating them as useful members of society. Thus, although
Small Harbour has outlived its usefulness, it continues to exist largely
because of the welfare and rehabilitation programmes of modern society.
Many people in Small Harbour have adopted a welfare-oriented strategy:
they are able to remain in the community because they are supported
by various forms of social assistance. Others derive a large portion of
their income from the rehabilitation programmes themselves. At least one
"fisherman" supports himself by attending Fisheries College in St. John's
each year. In addition to his board and lodging, he is paid a salary which
helps support his family through the rest of the year. As a result, he has
not needed to fish for several years. Other residents take advantage of
similar "upgrading" programmes available from trades schools across the
province. They learn to be carpenters, plumbers or heavy equipment
operators—skills which are of little use to them in Small Harbour. While
such courses obviously are intended to rehabilitate them for useful

employment outside, the salaries that they pay to students allow many Small Harbour men to remain where they are a little while longer. In this way they have been able to transform outside forces normally beyond their control into programmes in line with their own goals and values. But even with these new skills, their dependence on outside forces is so great that most were unable to suggest any local initiatives which could increase the number of jobs available on the island. Almost everyone looked directly to the government to plan and provide for his future.

The type of development that most concerns centralized government is the *top-down* variety which focuses on general strategies and rarely reaches the level of the small community. These development plans are directed towards major industrial complexes which provide large numbers of jobs quickly. In contrast *bottom-up* planning focuses on assisting community members, helping them design feasible projects, and training them in the managerial skills necessary to carry them out. It also provides the usually modest funds which make such local operations successful.

But there is more involved in this distinction between the two types of planning than the point of departure and the direction taken. They also differ in the extent to which they focus on the social and cultural dimensions of community life. Top-down planners seem inclined to focus on economic and industrial development, ignoring the consequences of their actions on social and cultural values. In contrast, those who orient their planning towards community development are more likely to focus on the effect that planning is having on the existing pattern of life.

At the time of this study there was no bottom-up planning taking place in Small Harbour. Although the community council had been formed and perhaps had the potential to develop managerial skills, it was simply a means to plead for favours in the name of the community. Until recently the only government plans which in any way affected the community were those related to industrialization and resettlement. These were directed towards phasing out the community, not developing it. Even though the government had made major efforts to improve the quality of living in Small Harbour, there was really no evidence to indicate that it was concerned with developing the community's employment prospects. Until that happens the people of Small Harbour will still have to go away to work. Those residents who think otherwise are only deluding themselves by mistaking improvements in quality of living for change in the community's ability to sustain life.

There is a major discrepancy between two sets of outlooks and values—the attitudes of the planners and the attitudes of the "planned". Most planners, particularly those who favour top-down, industrial development, are inclined to regard rural communities as archaic vestiges of a dying way of life. Even those planners who are oriented towards preserving rural communities are prone to condemn a village if it can no longer demonstrate that it is economically viable. On the other hand, many residents of Small Harbour and communities like her are so committed to their way of life that they would prefer to commute to work for much of the year rather than move. They are willing to delude themselves into thinking that changes in the cosmetics of community life are really changes in its fundamental economic structure. If we are to resolve this discrepancy, we must begin to investigate the criteria from which these conflicting attitudes arise. We must begin to develop a framework of concepts and tools whereby we can judge the viability of rural life.

I would argue that such a framework must start with a distinction between the criteria of *economic viability* and those which I will call *social vitality*. Most regional and community planning is based almost solely on economic criteria. Obviously a strong case can be made for the primacy of economic considerations in economic and regional development. Only when people have satisfied their basic needs for food, clothing and shelter can they begin to think in terms of human excellence. I do not argue that we should neglect economic concerns, or that economic disparity should not be a central consideration in any strategy of regional planning. My concern is that most regional planners seem to focus almost exclusively on economic considerations and that they neglect to consider the social structure, culture and values of the people for whom they are planning. Their conclusion that a community is no longer economically viable leads them to ignore the social fabric of community life.

Economic planners will hasten to point out that most good works of regional and community planning devote considerable space to the "social-factors" in development. Indeed, they do. But such social factors are usually considered obstacles to be overcome or altered if the economic policies are to be successful. One of the clearest expressions of this viewpoint is to be found in the opening address of the president of the Development Centre of the United Nations Organization for Economic Co-operation and Development (OECD) at its annual conference in 1966. Speaking on the relationship between economics and the other social sciences, he says:

... the economic sciences study rather the "necessary"—that is to say what should theoretically allow the fastest development, and that *the social and human sciences study the "possible", that is to say the social and psychological resistance which may manifest itself, and thus make it possible to discover ways and means of overcoming it.* (OECD, 1967:12, emphasis mine)

This approach is used only slightly more frequently than that which begins with a broad statement concerning the inseparability of economic and social development, and then proceeds to ignore social considerations throughout the remainder of the work.

I propose that in addition to criteria of economic viability, we should judge rural and community life in terms of some criteria of social vitality. One of the main reasons why planning based on economic considerations is more common than planning based on social considerations is that the criteria of economic disparity are obvious and easily measured. It is much more difficult to determine whether a region or community is socially disadvantaged.

What are the criteria of social vitality? The social vitality of a community operates on two levels. The institutions and organizations which formalize on-going daily activity and which structure social life constitute the *formal level of community social vitality.* These include the institutions of socialization and social control (Martindale 1962, 1963, 1966). In a small rural community the institutions of socialization are usually represented by the organizations of the family, the school and the church. The institutions of social control include everything from informal gossip to a formalized community council. These two institutional areas complement the economic institutions of a community or society and are integrated with them. If the observer focuses solely on economic viability, he ignores two equally important aspects of the institutional structure of a society.

Underlying the formal institutional level there is an *informal level of community social vitality.* Here the focus is on the *attitudes and values* of the community members and on their *involvement and committment* to community life. It is impossible to overestimate the importance of these factors in community life. Without the involvement and committment of its members, the institutions of a community could and would not function. In a community such as Small Harbour where economic viability has all but disappeared, it is often only the committment of the community members which maintains the community. Furthermore, this focus on committment and involvement provides an insight into two other important dimensions of community life; *the pattern of leadership* and the *extent of community co-operation.* Both are reflections of the committment and involvement of community members, and both are important measures of the social vitality of a community.

At the formal level, the social vitality of Small Harbour shows signs of considerable distress. Most of the traditional organizations have ceased to function: churches have closed; the Orange Lodge no longer dominates social life; the children must go away to school; the men must go away to work. The only people left in the community are the women and younger children, the elderly, the shopkeepers and teachers, the ne'er-do-wells, and those few men who are still able to obtain a living by combining fishing with some other activity. But there are some hopeful signs. A community council has been formed and a new church has replaced the old. Although the community has experienced considerable decline, one must be careful not to mistake the normal process of change for disintegration.

An examination of the informal level of social vitality provides a more detailed picture of life in Small Harbour. There can be no doubt that many residents are committed to the community. They do not want to move and many choose to migrate back and forth between home and work rather than to leave permanently. It became apparent from our conversations and interviews that the values and attitudes of almost all of these people are directed towards remaining in Small Harbour if possible, and certainly towards rural living rather than urban life.

The extent of community members' involvement in community affairs is less obvious. From our analysis there would appear to be two somewhat overlapping spheres of involvement. The first is the community council which is controlled by an elite group dominated by one or two individuals. The other sphere of activity centres around the new church. Most of the people who originally encouraged this church to come to the community were not among the community elite. Since members of the elite were committed to the older churches and held most of the lay offices in them, they could not easily transfer their allegiance to the new body. Thus the new church provided previously uninvolved community residents with a chance to become leaders in a community organization. But it is doubtful that this situation will be permanent: the comments of the traditional community leaders indicate that they are beginning to accept the new church, and some may "move over" and begin to occupy its leadership positions.

This discussion of community involvement has already led us to consider some aspects of the pattern of leadership and the extent of co-operation in Small Harbour. The two factors are interrelated. Strong and capable leadership is desirable in any community. It is particularly necessary in a community like Small Harbour which has little economic viability and where a strong effort is necessary if the community is to be able to persist. Yet strong leadership has a hidden danger. If the leaders of a community are too strong, too dictatorial or too self interested, they are unlikely to obtain the co-operation of community members, and co-operation is necessary if rural communities are to survive. Only then can they resist the pressures from outside which are aimed at their resettlement rather than their redevelopment.

It is extremely difficult to assess the quality of leadership and co-operation in Small Harbour. It would seem to be a mistake to regard the community council as a co-operative community effort. Although it was elected by the majority of the population, it appears to have operated as an elite group. On the other hand there can be little doubt that some of these leaders essentially "saved" the community through their canny use of the mass media. It is also obvious that virtually the whole community supported these actions.

If the community council is to be truly successful, it must begin to play an active part in more facets of community life. Instead of simply petitioning the government for services and facilities, it should encourage a general spirit of community co-operation whereby local residents can begin to develop new facilities and sources of employment themselves. This type of leadership and co-operation was conspicuously missing in Small Harbour and unlikely to be achieved in the future. Historically, there has been no strong spirit of intra-community co-operation in Newfoundland. The basic relational tie between merchant and fisherman was more like that between squire and peasant than that between relative equals. Fishing itself was organized on a family basis and, if anything, there was a state of controlled conflict between rival family groups. This may explain in part the failure of the co-operative movement in Newfoundland. It certainly suggests that Small Harbour and her sister communities are unlikely to be receptive to a movement involving co-operation.

Thus, even though it was the one community in all of Newfoundland to proclaim that it was "here to stay", Small Harbour is faced with an uncertain future. In the economic sphere it has declined to the point that there is now virtually no employment base. The community is so small that the emigration of a few families would probably result in the evacuation of the community. Even if it should remain, its survival beyond the present adult generation is in doubt. As long as there is no work, and as long as most parents encourage their children to leave, the community will remain on the verge of extinction. The main signs of revival are in the sphere of formal social vitality. The new council and new church have the potential to rebuild Small Harbour's social and economic life, but this requires a whole new approach to leadership and a new spirit of co-operation. The best that can be said is that most residents are still committed to their community and would like to remain.

But while Small Harbour's future must be considered precarious, it would be a mistake to believe that all rural communities are in similar straights. Even communities which outsiders consider to be without economic viability may be considered by local residents to be both economically viable and socially vital places in which to live. Their residents are absolutely convinced that "there's no better place" for them. Two prime examples are Mountain Cove and Grande Terre.

CHAPTER IV

MOUNTAIN COVE

Q.   Will persons now living within the proposed [national park] boundaries have to move?

A.   The National Parks Service have suggested that all families living between Rocky Harbour and Cow Head (total pop. about 600) be removed by 1973; that Sally's Cove (pop. 1966 census: 250) be removed by 1976; *and that Mountain Cove (pop. 1966 census about 700) be removed by 1979.* However, there is no final decision. The removal of Sally's Cove and Mountain Cove is under negotiation as they are considered by the Province to be potential assets to the national park. (Newfoundland, 1970b, emphasis mine)

"They was going to move Mountain Cove for the park"

Mountain Cove lies nestled between the ocean and the mountains on Newfoundland's west coast in the general area known as Bonne Bay. It is near Poplar Point, the major community on Bonne Bay, and is seventy miles by winding gravel road from the Trans Canada Highway.

The Bonne Bay area is renowned for its beauty. Gros Morne, one of Newfoundland's highest peaks, can be seen from almost anywhere along the bay, and the territory abounds with rich forest stands, while rivers and lakes fill almost every valley. The Newfoundland and Canadian governments have spent over a decade formulating plans for a national park in the area.[1] Most local residents were expected to approve of the park as it would provide a source of employment. But when the Government of Newfoundland published a white paper outlining its plans in April 1970, the residents were shocked to discover that their way of life was threatened. Most of the communities near the park were slated to be "removed", and Mountain Cove was one of the communities listed.

[1] National parks in Canada are federally financed and operated. Thus the new park would entail a considerable federal investment in the area. In return the province would have to cede all mineral and forest rights within the park boundaries.

My first impression of Mountain Cove was of its incredible beauty. After a drive through a bare mountain valley, the road emerged high above the ocean. Down below an expanse of rocky beach separated a row of houses from the sparkling azure sea. In the distance to the south of the village a river flowed beside a hill. A few small boats clustered in the mouth of the river which formed a small natural harbour. Here the row of houses turned to retrace the course of the river and stopped just short of a glittering blue expanse of lake. Even from this distance the village appeared larger than most rural Newfoundland communities. The houses were three and four rows deep along the bank of the river. Above the community was a large verdant plateau where vegetables grew in small fenced plots and a few cattle grazed contentedly. Green grazing land lay at the end of the lake which faded into the mountains in the distance.

As I approached the community I realized that I had been misled. Although nature has endowed the area with unsurpassed beauty, the village itself could hardly be described as picturesque. Mountain Cove provides a striking contrast to most Newfoundland rural communities with their picture-postcard, brightly painted houses. The houses are small, cluttered together and often unpainted. The following description taken from my notes after my first drive through the community indicates the extent of my disenchantment.

> The first impression one gets on entering the community is poverty. . . . Its houses are built primarily along the beach and along the narrow road that runs between the houses and the fish stages lining the beach. . . . Only a few houses in the community show signs of any affluence, or even of neatness, tidiness, cleanliness or paint.

> Mountain Cove is one of the most depressed looking communities I have seen in Newfoundland. This is all the more surprising considering its size which must place it amongst the largest fifty or sixty communities in the province.

Mountain Cove looks even more depressed in contrast to Poplar Point which one must travel through to reach it. Poplar Point is a community of old, stately homes set off by rows of tall poplars which give it the appearance of a quaint English country town. Although smaller than Mountain Cove, Poplar Point (1971 population: 500) seems larger because it is the administrative centre for the area and has a post office, town hall, library, magistrate's office, welfare office,

RCMP detachment headquarters, telegraph office, handicraft store, tourist information centre and restaurant. It is also the home base for both the Anglican and United Church clergy serving the region. It lacks only a resident doctor, for the area's medical facilities are based in a small hospital across the bay.

Although Mountain Cove is the largest community in the whole area, it has few facilities. It has no tourist facilities and no restaurants other than some "pop and french fries" operations which are referred to locally as "parlours". The major signs of provincial government investment are a small breakwater at the mouth of the river, a post office and a large, modern high school.

The contrast is obvious. Poplar Point is old, comfortable, picturesque and an administrative centre. Mountain Cove is ugly, unkempt and unrewarded. While Poplar Point was destined by the park planners to remain and become a centre of local activity, Mountain Cove was to be "removed". Obviously in the view of these protectors of beauty, there could be no salvation for such an eyesore.

"The French used to fish here"

The decision to "remove" Mountain Cove is the latest incident in a history of government harassment. The origins of Mountain Cove are very different from those of Small Harbour. The community is relatively young: many of the residents remember the first permanent settlers, and the oldest living residents settled in the community when there were only half a dozen families there. At the time of the earliest census record (1874) the community had only twenty-six inhabitants, thirteen of whom were under ten years of age. All of these early residents had been born in Newfoundland and belonged to the Church of England. Little else is known about them.

But while Mountain Cove itself has little recorded history, it is in an area which has been the subject of international comment for over two centuries. Mountain Cove lay on the "French Shore" as defined by the Treaty of Utrecht of 1713. Under this agreement France gave up all rights to permanent settlement in Newfoundland in return for a British guarantee that French fishermen could have summer fishing rights along nearly half of the Newfoundland coast, including the area around Mountain Cove. The French immediately began to "take matters into their own hands by hustling British fishermen and merchants off the treaty coast" (Thompson, 1961:19). Under the Treaty of Versailles in 1783, the French fishing territory was changed to include the whole of Newfoundland's west coast where there were few British settlers. In return France gave up her fishing rights to a segment of the northeast coast where there was considerable British immigration.[2] At this time the British agreed to have their settlements within the French fishing territory "removed" (Thompson, 1961:192).

This agreement initiated a long period during which the British government harassed her own subjects on Newfoundland's west coast. As a result of "complaints from St. John's and Paris against each other's lobster fishery", the British passed "the lobster act of 1878" which gave the colonial government the power to prohibit lobster fishing in the colony (Thompson, 1961:94), including the area around Mountain Cove. Several older residents gave dramatic accounts of British harassment around the turn of the century.

> I seen it where the fishermen here had cases of lobster hid away
> in order to keep them from being destroyed [by British naval men].

The British reportedly had a patrol ship, *The Buzzard*, stationed in Bonne Bay which frequently raided Mountain Cove. In one such raid the men of the community hid in the woods, but the British captured many of them, broke all their lobster boilers and destroyed as much of their catch as they could find. They carried off many Mountain Cove men and threatened to take them to St. John's for trial, leaving their families to face possible starvation. Fortunately they were taken instead to Bonne Bay and released after a few days. We were told how the men then walked home overland and immediately began intensive lobster fishing in order to recover their losses.

Despite this harsh treatment the community grew by approximately 100 people each decade until it was much larger than most Newfoundland villages.[3] Perhaps this was because Mountain Cove provided ample opportunities for earning a livelihood.

The community lies near a rich offshore fishing ground known locally as Green Bank and the basis of life is the fishery. Originally the French fished from "bateaus" which they moored in the river. Later the British fished during the summer from small boats which could be pulled up on

[2] The territory in which Small Harbour is located was in this area.

[3] The most rapid growth has been since 1904 when all French fishing rights in the area ended. Since 1960 the population has remained relatively constant at between 650 and 700 persons.

the beach because the entrance to the river was too shallow to permit large boats to enter during low tide. Since Mountain Cove is in a lush river valley with good soil for crops and for grazing cattle, it became a supplier of fresh meat throughout the area.

> A cruel lot of it was taken to Bonne Bay and shipped all up and down the coast.

Lumbering, too, provided a major source of income. The hills behind Mountain Cove contain some of Newfoundland's finest forest reserves and one informant estimated that as recently as ten years ago some 600,000 feet of lumber would be piled by the lake after the spring run-off. During the last thirty years prospecting for minerals has been a source of employment as several prospecting crews have used local residents as cooks and guides.

Although it grew rapidly, the community was slow to acquire public facilities. Local residents talked of an early church erected over 100 years ago, but there is no census record of any church prior to 1911 when the community had both a Church of England and a Methodist chapel. Before this Mountain Cove received spiritual guidance from itinerant preachers who walked over the mountains to visit their congregations. [4] By 1921 the community also had a Salvation Army church and the population was divided almost equally between the three denominations. This religious balance has been maintained to the present.[5] Schools were even slower to appear. There were no children attending classes prior to 1901, and no school in the community until just before 1911. Today Mountain Cove has three churches with separate primary schools to serve the needs of each congregation, and a new "integrated" high school for all three denominations. Logging and lumbering have declined and fishing once again has come to dominate the economic life of the community.

To find out how the residents of Mountain Cove lived, and particularly to learn how they reacted to the threat of removal, I spent several weeks in the community. During this time I formally interviewed many household heads and talked informally with members of many other households.

---

[4] The most famous of these men was Parson Curling, who was based in Birchy Cove (now renamed Curling) over sixty miles away and served the area for many years.

[5] A special census tabulation for 1961 shows 266 Anglican, 255 Salvation Army, and 170 United Church adherents.

Those interviewed included twenty-three representatives of the general population selected at random and three people who were leaders in the community. Unlike Small Harbour there were only three people in our original sample who had moved, were away working, or who had died. A number of people could not be interviewed: two persons flatly refused; three agreed to be interviewed but kept postponing the actual date; and five indicated their willingness to be interviewed but were "too busy at the fish" whenever we called on them. While there were very few of our sample absent from the community, a larger proportion were unwilling to be interviewed than in Small Harbour.

Every one of the men and sixteen of the twenty-two wives in our sample were born in Mountain Cove. It is unusual to find such a high rate of endogamous marriage: most rural Newfoundlanders marry persons from nearby villages. The high rate in Mountain Cove may be an indication of the social isolation of the community or it may simply be a consequence of its larger size.[6]

The household heads we interviewed were slightly younger than those in Small Harbour with a mean age of 41.6 years. This may not be an accurate reflection of the age of the population because many of those we were unable to interview were younger men who were busy fishing. Of those we did interview, eleven were actively engaged in the fishery and another five were retired fishermen. In addition we interviewed two merchants, two persons who were otherwise employed and six persons whose only income was government assistance. The educational level of our sample was much poorer than in Small Harbour: only three persons had gone beyond grade seven and only one had finished high school. Mountain Cove appears to be a traditional fishing community where boys leave school as soon as possible to work in the fishing boats. In recent years this pattern has continued and, as in the past, there seems to be little value placed on acquiring an education.

"I don't believe there are two worries in Mountain Cove among everybody"

Mountain Cove is unique among neighbouring communities. Not only does it look different but, according to those people from Poplar Point who come in frequent contact with Mountain Cove residents, its people also behave differently and have different values. Many of these out-

---

[6]Marriage outside the community has the obvious function of avoiding incest taboos in small rural communities where families are already closely interrelated. This may not be such a problem in a community as large as Mountain Cove.

siders are government officials who have an unattractive image of the
Mountain Cove way of life. One welfare officer described it as "a traditional welfare community", and estimated that some 60 percent of the
population was in receipt of able-bodied relief. Most outsiders saw the
people of Mountain Cove as diffident, difficult and unco-operative. In
the words of one of them:

> They're the stubbornest people I ever met. Anything going to
> change Mountain Cove will not only meet opposition, but
> everything else.

Not all outsiders regarded the community with suspicion. A local cleric
gave a warmer interpretation of the qualities of Mountain Cove residents.
He described them as being "kind, friendly and carefree".

> Nobody there worries about anything. I don't believe there
> are two worries in Mountain Cove among everybody.

From either perspective the people of Mountain Cove seem to have a
distinct culture, unique within the region and within Newfoundland
generally. At their worst they appear to outsiders as hostile and unco-
operative, at their best, independent and easy going.

Although outsiders give the impression that Mountain Cove is a
"welfare ghetto" full of people unwilling to work, just the opposite picture emerges when one talks to the residents themselves. Most talk
incessantly of the vast quantitites of fish caught locally and use this to
indicate both their industry and the solid economic base of their community. I was told repeatedly that 1,350,000 pounds of fish had been
shipped out of the community the previous year. This was obviously a
source of considerable community pride as well as a topic of general
conversation.

The residents of Mountain Cove see themselves as the only self-
sufficient, hard working community in the district. They were critical
of another large fishing community near Bonne Bay which was reportedly
"doing poorly with the fish". They heaped scorn on most residents of the
bay area because most Bonne Bay communities are too far up the bay to
make fishing profitable, and their economy is based primarily on a
logging industry which has gone into decline.

> They're living a lot better here than those in the woods of
> Bonne Bay.

But their greatest contempt was reserved for the inhabitants of Poplar
Point.

People in Poplar Point condemn the residents of Mountain Cove for being "on welfare". In return people from Mountain Cove think that Poplar Point is being supported by the government because many Poplar Point residents are government employees. They make virtually no distinction between being "on welfare" and working for the government, and think less of government employees than of those who must supplement "honest toil" with welfare assistance.

> In Poplar Point . . . one-third is working with the government and the rest is merchants.

> Nobody works in there. There's only welfare and government jobs. You always see them out here looking for their halibut and fish.

> Three parts that's in there is getting a government salary.

> The only difference between here and Poplar Point is that there's a dozen and a half government people there.

> I'd live better here than in Poplar Point. The people there has to come here for a fish. That's the last place I'd go on the island.

One possible reason for this rather unusual outlook could be the long tradition of political patronage in Newfoundland. In the past many government workers were given their jobs as "handouts" either for service to the political party in power, or because of kin and friendship ties with key politicians.[7] Given this, it really does not seem all that unusual to consider government employment a form of welfare assistance.

According to many Mountain Cove residents, the community of Poplar Point would virtually disappear if the government withdrew its personnel, for it has little other economic base. They indicated that only two or three persons fished from Poplar Point even though it is not substantially farther from the fishing grounds than Mountain Cove. In contrast, Mountain Cove is firmly rooted in the fishery and its residents claim that they could survive even under the harshest conditions. But the crux of their argument is that Poplar Point makes no contribution to the economy of Newfoundland and drains it of scarce dollars, while Mountain Cove residents through their fishing bring new dollars into the economy. It simply did not make sense to them that Mountain Cove was slated to be "removed" and Poplar Point was permitted to remain.

This assessment of themselves vis-a-vis Poplar Point is based on the Mountain Cove residents' belief that they are hard working and industri-

---

[7] For a detailed discussion of Newfoundland politics and patronage see Matthews, 1974 and Noel, 1971.

ous fishermen. There is an obvious conflict between their statements concerning their industry and those of the local welfare official who described them as virtually unwilling to work. My interviews ultimately led me to believe that both statements contained some truth.

I reached this conclusion after several of my informants volunteered the information that some Mountain Cove people were able to collect welfare assistance at the same time as they were actively fishing. One of them labelled this process "fishing crosshanded". According to him, a man may have one or two men fishing with him on his boat who do not register their catch for unemployment insurance benefits. Instead the man who owns the boat sells all the fish in his name and alone becomes eligible for benefits. The others on the boat are then free to tell the welfare officer in Poplar Point that they have no income and are therefore eligible for welfare. Later they can split the income from the fish, the welfare payments and the unemployment insurance receipts among all parties "and there is no way of checking against it". The same sort of information came from a variety of residents.

> There's men fishing and getting big money and going in every month getting their dole. I worked everywhere at everything.

> You take for instance I made twenty dollars [fishing] today and every day its calm. And then the others here can do this and also go to the welfare officer.

> There are fishermen here who stays ashore welfare days to get their cheque instead of making a living. Something should be done about it. . . . Any person who got a boat can make a living here without going to the welfare officer.

> They makes the money. Puts it in their children's name or puts it in their money boxes. And then they goes on the dole. It's cruel [awfully common] here.

One person even indicated that a similar practice takes place in other economic activities.

> People here sold a thousand dollars worth of beef last year and put it in their young fellow's [son's] name, and went on relief.

It would be wrong to conclude from this that all residents of Mountain Cove are engaged in cheating the government. Those who told me about the practice usually professed to be hard working fishermen who were upset by the behaviour of their neighbours. But it is further evidence of a very unusual value pattern: the residents manage to maintain the values of hard work and industry at the same time as they accept welfare payments. Given their description of Poplar Point, it would seem that they regard this as a more "honest" form of earning a livelihood than working for the government and thus being dependent on it for all of their income.

Those who might be inclined to moralize and disapprove of such behaviour should not do so before they are fully aware of the regulations governing the payment of unemployment insurance to fishermen. Unlike most other workmen, fishermen are essentially self-employed and only seasonally occupied. When unemployment insurance was made available to fishermen, the government was concerned that many fishermen might sit back and catch little if they could collect benefits based on the number of months worked. In an attempt to prevent this the government made unemployment insurance benefits to fishermen conditional on the amount of fish they caught. If they did not catch a certain minimum, they were ineligible for benefits.

To the government this was a perfectly rational way of keeping people from being paid benefits for doing little work. However it wrought incredible hardship on those fishermen who worked hard throughout the fishing season but, because of poor fish stocks or bad weather conditions, were still unable to obtain the minimum catch that would qualify them for unemployment insurance benefits. Despite their hard work, they had both a low income and no cash assistance during the winter. They were doubly cursed.

To the fisherman the system of "fishing crosshanded" is a perfectly legitimate way of ensuring that this rarely happens. By declaring all the fish in one man's name, a crew can be certain that at least one member of the boat will be eligible for benefits. When this man has reached the necessary minimum to qualify for winter assistance, they can then begin to record all their catch in another man's name. They hope that as the season progresses all the crew will be able to qualify for assistance. If not, they have protected themselves against the terrible possibility that no one in the crew will qualify for government help through the winter.

There is still another way to justify this practice. In my commentary on Small Harbour I argued that that community continues to exist only because it has become a *client of modernization.* Small Harbour residents have managed to adopt a welfare adaptive strategy: they have learned to use various welfare and rehabilitation programmes designed to train them for useful work outside the community as sources of income which enable them to remain where they are. Mountain Cove residents use welfare payments in much the same way. But instead of simply becoming *adaptive* to welfare as was the case in Small Harbour, they have used welfare in an *integrative* way. The distinction here is between a passive dependence on welfare and the active use of welfare to supplement their regular economic activity. In order to survive Mountain Cove men must earn a living from a variety of sources including fishing, mining, logging and farming. Government assistance is regarded simply as another source of income to be "harvested". The implications of this for the economic viability of the community will be discussed in more detail in the commentary at the end of the chapter.

Different values and different behaviour patterns tend to isolate Mountain Cove residents socially from those in neighbouring communities. It is understandable that many outsiders mistakenly regard Mountain Cove, with its poor housing and high incidence of welfare, as a typical welfare ghetto full of impoverished and demoralized men, but nothing seems farther from the truth.

Most Mountain Cove residents are quick to point out the relative ease with which they can make a good living. They have the plentiful fish stocks in the area virtually to themselves, and when asked to indicate what they "liked best" about the community twenty of twenty-six householders mentioned the easy availability of fish.

> I like the fishery and they catch a lot of fish here.

> I'd sooner be here than anywhere else in the world. It's lovely scenery here and there are a lot of fishermen here. Three-quarters of them makes their living at it and gets a very good price.

Many of these people also noted the ready availability of other sources of livelihood.

> Well, you can grow your own vegetables and keep your own sheep and catch your own fish and lobster.

> I say they lives better here on accounts you got all your fresh fish and meats and butter, milk and cream. Most people here have their own vegetables.

> I loves fishing and on the water. And I likes hunting. And its all pretty good here.

> They got their own vegetables here and they rear their own meat.

> I likes keeping cattle. It's all I done ever since I was a boy.

Still others commented on the peace and tranquility.

> It's very quiet and clean and the people are nice. You can always jump aboard your boat and get a fresh fish, lobster or halibut.

> There's nice fresh air here. It's not polluted here by factories anyway. And I loves the fishing and on the water. And I likes hunting pretty good, and its pretty good here.

But the most interesting insight into the ease of making a living from all sources came from the man who said:

> It's so good a place as there is around the island. Anyone who is working has no trouble to make a living here. You can make a living here one day and make a hundred dollars. And then the next day you can go to Bonne Bay and get another hundred dollars [from the Welfare Officer].

I do not mean to suggest by this that the residents of Mountain Cove are rich, or that they live particularly well for they do not. Like most Newfoundland fishermen they manage to "get by". If they have any additional money it is spent primarily on alcohol. One person suggested that some men use their welfare assistance for basic food stuffs and the money they earn for beer.

> Forty percent go fishing not to earn a living but to get beer money. They go to the welfare officer for food.

His comments were one further indication of the "carefree" attitude of Mountain Cove residents.

"The people of Mountain Cove, one won't trust the other one"

The unique value system of Mountain Cove residents shows, too, in the attitudes they have toward one another and in the social structure of their community. Mountain Cove was isolated until the road from Poplar Point was constructed thirteen years ago. The community is no longer geographically isolated, but it remains socially isolated. Few residents have much to do with nearby communities. Seven of the household heads we interviewed had not been out of the community in the preceding twelve months even though a small bus travels back and forth to Poplar Point several times each day. Four others had been only as far as Poplar Point, and nine had been no farther than the city of Corner Brook about 100 miles away. Most of these latter visits were brief trips to consult welfare officials or to visit the hospital. Four other persons had visited friends and relatives in other nearby communities. Only two of our sample had travelled outside the region, one to eastern New-foundland for a vacation and one to Ontario in a futile search for work.

This isolation combined with their distinctive values might lead one to expect that the people of Mountain Cove form a highly cohesive group. To determine whether this was the case we asked our sample of household heads a series of questions dealing with the degree of community satisfaction, some of which required them to evaluate their relationships with other members of the community. Their answers revealed that most had strong personal friendships within the community, but that, in general, the community lacks any real sense of cohesiveness. Only two of our respondents indicated that there was no one in the community they could call on for help in time of need, and only five felt that "real friends are hard to find" there. But twenty-three out of twenty-six respondents claimed that, "It is difficult for the people here to get together on anything."

Mountain Cove residents are aware of this lack of cohesiveness and co-operation and feel strongly about it. In response to our question about what the people could do to improve the community "if they were willing to work together as a group", half listed the things which could be done, but doubted that the community would ever co-operate to do them, while the other half launched into long diatribes about the total impossibility of community members co-operating on anything. In doing so they often revealed their own mistrust of their neighbours.

> The people of Mountain Cove, one won't trust the other one, and we've got too many that steal anything they can walk away with.
>
> I don't say the people will get together much here. . . . I don't say the people here would do a five minute job for anyone else for a dollar.
>
> The people here . . . if one wants to do something the other goes against him.
>
> As a matter of fact they're not going to get together.
>
> If they could get together and work together they could make a living. But our people won't do that today.
>
> If they could get together, they could get a breakwater. . . . But it's the getting them together here that's the problem.
>
> There's nothing here but fishermen. If they had those longliners like the couple here, they'd do better. There is fellows here can

> build them themselves. But they'd have to get together as a group
> in order to do that, wouldn't they!

> That'll never happen. . . . You'll never get the people together.
> They all work for themselves.

> That's the one thing that's wrong with the place. . . . People can't
> work together.

> That's our whole problem. We can't come together. They won't
> co-operate together like.

Several of these respondents recalled an ill-fated co-operative store that had
once opened in the community. It was plagued by mismanagement problems and twice destroyed by fire.

> It's a job to get them together. We had a co-op for a few years
> and then they started up their shops.

From these comments it would appear that the lack of co-operation
in Mountain Cove actually borders on mistrust and open hostility. If the
community members cannot get together on anything, who then runs
the community? Almost unanimously the residents picked two leaders.
One person was named as a leader by twenty-three and a second person,
by fourteen. No other resident was suggested as a leader by more than
four persons.

The leader named by almost every respondent was an older man who
had lived most of his life in the community. He had served in the armed
forces in Europe during the First World War, had been a carpenter in
several Newfoundland centres during the 1930s and had worked for
several years as a guide and foreman for prospecting and mining companies operating in the Mountain Cove area. Although he had never been
a merchant in the traditional sense, in recent years he had been the agent
in the community for a major brewery. He was particularly respected for
his war service and he was actively involved in the Canadian Legion. In
addition he lived in "one of the better homes" and had "kept his place
in the community and brought his family up right". During this time he
had been an active participant in all facets of community life. This is
borne out by the comments of his fellow citizens whose remarks provide
an exceptional insight into the traditional role of an outport community
leader.

> No matter who dies they [the family] goes to Mr. _____ for help.
> And if he hears of anyone dying he's always there to see that every-
> thing is under way and there's nothing left out. Mr. _____ is the

president of the Legion and he's the mayor and he's in the Orange
Lodge. Everything that's going on he's got an office in I guess.

If you went to him for advice you'd be able to get some sensible
information.

He's a man we've always looked up to to get things done, even in
sickness and death, and in the churches and schools and things like
that.

When something needed to be done about the roads he was always
the first to write in [to the government] about it.

Mr. _____ is always there if anyone dies or if you wanted a casket.
He's been looking after the community and have done a lot of work
around through here. As far as I can see he knows more and is older.
As long as I can remember he's been building caskets and laying out
people. That's how I come to pitch on him.

So well is he ensconced in his leadership position that one person simply
replied, "[He] is not a leader. He is king."

The second man frequently mentioned as a community leader was
the son of the largest store owner in the community. After graduating
from high school he had worked for several years in the city. Eight years
before our study he had returned to his birthplace and had taken over
the family business from his aging father. He was a relatively young man
and the basis of his leadership role was very different from that of the
other leader. To a considerable extent he was a community leader because he was the dominant village merchant, but he was also better
educated than most and had gained managerial experience when he
worked away from the community. Like the older man he had been
active in community affairs since his return.

Both of these leaders had gained their positions in traditional ways.
One had given a lifetime of community service, the other was the largest
community merchant. In recent years they had formalized their leadership positions through active involvement in a newly-formed community
council. This organization appears to have been the inspiration of a hard-
driving community teacher who had since left the community. At the
time of our study the older man was its chairman or mayor, while the
younger man held the position of secretary-treasurer. The situation is
analogous to that which existed in Small Harbour. Both communities
have councils which are dominated by the same people who would have
power without this formal body. But in Mountain Cove the leaders
actually hold the formal leadership positions within their council.

It is natural for the traditional community leaders to dominate a community council, particularly during its early years. The merchants are often the only ones with the necessary education, administrative skills and experience to undertake many administrative activities. Moreover they are probably the only persons with networks to outside governmental agencies. In Newfoundland traditional leaders perform two major functions. They are expected to be involved in the daily activities of the community, particularly in time of crisis, and to represent their community to the outside world. Thus it is often the merchant who contacts an acquaintance in the Department of Education to ensure that the community has a steady supply of teachers, or the political representative for the area to lobby for necessary public works. Communities can become so dependent on their leaders that some have actually been forced to resettle when the merchant has closed shop and moved elsewhere. Without his help they could not obtain teachers or necessary public works. Few community councils could operate without the advice, expertise and contacts of the traditional community leaders.

In return for their participation, most leaders benefit from the formation of a community council. By holding public office they can legitimate their traditional power and make requests that are formally sanctioned by the people, even if these requests are of considerable benefit to themselves. Furthermore, communities which form councils are usually considered to be dynamic and progressive by government officials and are more likely to obtain various new amenities. These not only make the community a better place in which to live, but they usually provide construction jobs for community members. Much of the money they earn will ultimately reach the pockets of the local merchant.

The community council in Mountain Cove performs many more traditional civic functions than did its counterpart in Small Harbour. It sponsors regular garbage collection and supervises the upkeep of the village roads. It has provided some street lighting, constructed a community hall for dances and weddings, attempted to clean the beach of refuse and set up a soccer pitch in a rented field at the edge of town. Most of the money for these services is provided by the provincial government, but each householder is also taxed seven dollars per year.

Not all Mountain Cove residents co-operate with the council by paying these fees. Both the council leaders and some of the other citizens noted how difficult it was to collect this money. Short of bringing their neighbours to court, the council has few sanctions it can use. The power and authority of the traditional leaders is therefore likely to be very important in getting these debts paid.

The two men who appear to dominate life in Mountain Cove are not the only people with any influence in the community. Indeed, it would not be in keeping with the character of Moutain Cove to have only one or two leaders. At least a dozen others vie for power. Some of these are shopkeepers. Unlike most rural Newfoundland communities, Mountain Cove has nearly a dozen small business operations, including a number of small grocery stores, three or four "parlours" and brewers agents. Several respected fishermen, church leaders, senior citizens and a few younger men also have a following in the community. Most of these people have held seats on the council. Residents told of conflict among the various leadership factions and several were highly critical of some of these leaders and even of the council itself.

"Half of Brampton is Mountain Cove"

Mountain Cove is not without problems. The residents' unusual values and attitudes isolate them socially from nearby villages and foster mistrust and hostility within the community. There is no evidence of general community co-operation. Rather the community seems to be held together primarily through the efforts of a charismatic older leader and the main village merchant. Despite these problems, most residents maintained that they were satisfied with life in their community because it was relatively easy to make a living.

One of the main indicators of community satisfaction or dissatisfaction is the extent of migration out of a community. People move for both economic and social reasons. In Newfoundland most rural people move to find work so migration is an indication of economic problems. They also move in order to get better opportunities for their children— specifically, better education. Since schools train people for jobs, moves of this kind are motivated by a combination of economic and social factors.

Their comments on the general ease of earning a living in Mountain Cove would lead one to expect that most residents see little economic benefit in moving. Among those we interviewed this certainly proved to be the case. Most of the original sample still lived in the community and fifteen had never lived anywhere else. Of those who had lived elsewhere, five had been away for brief periods while working temporarily on boats or in lumber camps and only six had lived outside the community for longer than a year at any one time. They included three men who had been stationed in Europe during the wars, two who had worked in larger Newfoundland centres and one man who had worked in Ontario for about a year. This limited out-migration contrasts sharply with that of Small Harbour.

However the data these men provided on their siblings indicate that extensive migration from Mountain Cove has taken place in the past. Our sample had thirty-eight brothers living outside the community and only thirty-five brothers who still resided in it. In addition they had a total of forty-three sisters living elsewhere and only thirty living in the community. It appears that the rate of migration from Mountain Cove in the past has been almost as great as that of Small Harbour. Since few of those interviewed had ever lived elsewhere, it appears that those who migrate from Mountain Cove rarely return, or return only for short periods before leaving permanently, while those who remain behind seldom see the need to look for work outside the community. If this is the case, Mountain Cove is a perfect example of a community where the excess population is forced to move.

The migration picture becomes more complicated when we examine the moves made by the children of our respondents. Since the members of our sample were generally younger than those we interviewed in Small Harbour, they tended to have more small children living at home. They had a total of seventy-nine children under eighteen and all but one of these was at home. Of the forty-two children over the age of eighteen, twenty-five were living in the community and fifteen of these lived in the parental home.[8] Thus our sample had only eighteen children living outside Mountain Cove. Allowing for the difference in age and sample size of each community, we still find that the emigration of the present generation of young people from Mountain Cove is less than half that of Small Harbour. This suggests that either Mountain Cove's young adults are prepared to live with conditions which would be intolerable to the young people of Small Harbour, or that the problems which lead people to migrate are not as great as they are in Small Harbour. The evidence suggests that the latter is the case.

Although few people have left Mountain Cove in recent years, we heard repeated references to a pattern of migration extending from

[8]This latter group contained several married sons and daughters who had moved into their parents' house when they married.

Mountain Cove to Brampton, Ontario.[9] As one respondent explained:

> Half of Brampton is Mountain Cove. They've been going to
> Brampton since way back. The young towed the old and the
> rest died out.

Our data substantiate that this route has been common for some time.
Twenty-four of the respondents' siblings lived outside Newfoundland:
eight of these were in Brampton and eleven in nearby Toronto. Similarly
ten of the respondents' children lived outside Newfoundland, five in Brampton and three in Toronto. Thus the Brampton-Toronto area seems to have a
continuing attraction for those who move from Mountain Cove.[10]

In Small Harbour most residents were inclined to underestimate the
extent of out-migration. In Mountain Cove residents' estimates of the
extent of migration both into and out of the community varied widely,
ranging from none to fifteen families each way. Most maintained that
very few families had left the community and that only four or five had
come to settle after the men had married local girls. As in Small Harbour,
there was a general tendency to underestimate the extent of out-migration
by failing to include single people who had left and to claim as new
immigrants those former residents who had returned home to get married
and settle down in the community.

Unlike Small Harbour which was steadily dwindling, Mountain Cove
is a growing community of 700 persons. Most people stay in the community because it is easy to make a living from the fishery. One would
expect that parents would encourage their children to stay too. But
those who felt that their children should leave outnumbered those who
felt they should stay by twenty to six. Poor employment prospects was
the reason most often cited.

> If they got their education, what are they going to do here?

> No sir, they're most certainly not going to stay here. . . . Because
> there's not enough jobs available here. My boys aren't going to do
> what their father did in the fishing boat all his life.

[9]This is what demographers refer to as a "migration stream". Family members who
are already established elsewhere help and care for their newly-arrived relatives
until they can find a job and become established on their own. Thus over a period
of time a sizeable satellite community is established in the new place of residence.

[10]Some Mountain Cove residents may have difficulty distinguishing between Toronto
and Brampton and may have indicated relatives living in Toronto when these relatives actually live in nearby Brampton. For this reason we have included data on
migration to both cities. If our data are correct they suggest that males tend to
obtain work in Brampton, while female migrants are more likely to find work in
Toronto.

I don't think there's much for them to stay here, unless they're going fishing. So I imagine the best thing for them is to go away and find a job.

I don't think they should stay. I encouraged my daughters to leave here once they got their education. But any fellow that is satisfied to go fishing should stay.

If there's no more going on here when they grow up apart from the fishery, I think they should move.

Even many of those who wished their children to stay seemed to think this was a vain hope.

They should stay here if they had anything to work at. . . . But there's nothing.

It'll be all right for them to stay here if they find anything to do. . . . Fishing is about the only thing.

There's plenty of work here if they are good to work. But anybody who's no good to work is no good anywhere.

I think they should stay here if they got anything to do. Like if their fathers have a fit out for fishing.

Most residents do not wish their children to become fishermen, but there is no other alternative for them in Mountain Cove. Parents therefore encourage their children to get an education and seek a different kind of employment elsewhere. This does not so much reflect disatisfaction with the community as with fishing as a means of making a living.

"You've still got that hard work, but there's a better chance for a living"

With this synopsis of the history, value orientation, organization and migration pattern of Mountain Cove, we can assess how the residents of Mountain Cove view the changes which are taking place in their community and respond to the threat of resettlement.

All but two of our respondents were convinced that life in Mountain Cove had improved over the past fifteen or twenty years. They cited such changes as roads, electricity, better markets for their fish and improved farming conditions to substantiate their claim.

It's been improved a lot. About twenty years ago we hadn't anything around us: roads, lights, high school, community centre, breakwater. . . .

> We got all kinds of fish buyers here now. One time I had to give
> it away for six dollars a quintal [114 pounds].

> Its more kept and cleaner. And there's a little more industry on
> the part of some people with regards to farming.

The two persons who disagreed suggested that migration from the community had weakened it and that there was a lower moral standard
among those who remained.

But when asked if they themselves were living better now than twenty
years ago, the responses varied widely. A large majority felt that their
own lot in life had improved. Most pointed out that they had more
money and better food than in the past, but often added that they had
to work just as hard as before to get it.

> We have the privilege of getting more things to eat and better
> things to eat than we did years ago. Before the last ten or fifteen
> years no one had a deep-freeze in their stores and you couldn't
> get anything fresh. Now all these stores have a deep-freeze and
> you can get whatever you mind to buy.

> You still got that hard work, but there's a better chance for a
> living.

> I would say better, a lot better. As far as my family is concerned,
> we're working for a living and we still raise our own gardens. The
> main thing is you got a job and better schooling.

One long-time recipient of welfare was even grateful for the increase in
government assistance.

> You can get more now. The ones what's fishing, when they're not
> fishing, gets enough from the government to live off.

Four residents felt that living conditions for them were actually worse
than in the past. Two of these were fishermen, one was employed at other
work and the fourth was "on welfare". They cited the lack of work,
particularly for young people, the poor moral character of the people
and the difficulty of getting welfare assistance.

> I sees more money but I don't think me living is as good as
> twenty years ago. One time we had our own fish and vegetables.
> Now we don't have it because the other people steals it. We had
> to give up keeping sheep and gardens because the other people
> takes it.

> For the married man its better, but for the young it's not. Young
> men can't get relief.

When asked what they could do to improve their collective lot, few could suggest anything.

> I think I'd have a hard job to make a better living than I'm doing now.

> Not here. I don't see a thing I could start here. Not if you haven't got learning.

In all of the interviews the only suggestions were four fishermen's vague statements about the need for better fishing gear.

> If you had the boat and the fishing gear, you could make a good living here in Mountain Cove.

> I could have a better living fishing, if I had the rig to fish.

Two small storekeepers thought they could live better if they only had the capital to build larger operations.

> If we had the finance we'd go places. I like to work and I'd like the money to start a restaurant. I'd do something then that would be worthwile to the community.

The dilemma was the same as that which faced the people of Small Harbour. The community lacks the expertise, initiative and capital to undertake any real development. Like the residents of Small Harbour, they look to the government for development assistance. They simply know no other way.

Although they lacked ideas about ways to improve the community by co-operating among themselves, they had many suggestions of ways in which *the government* could improve the community. Most of these centered on the fishery.

> The government could do a lot. They could dredge out this river and build a breakwater. And they could give them a good motor to put in the boats they can build. They can make a damm good living here. They haven't *got* to go out of this place for a living if the government mind to do this.

> I think the government instead of feeding the people should buy ten or twelve big boats. Instead of feeding them, make them work for their food.

> If they had a breakwater here they would do all right. A little breakwater even 200 feet would make a lot of difference to this cove and the ice would never hurt them here. It should have been there forty years ago.[11]

[11] This is quite realistic. The fishermen of Mountain Cove carry on their trade under some of the most difficult conditions in Newfoundland. Their only harbour is the

It would be difficult to fault the people of Mountain Cove for their dependence on the government. While community-sponsored, self-help projects may be a desirable ideal, only the government has the capital and equipment to undertake the construction of breakwaters and harbours. If the people cannot turn to their elected government to help them with such tasks, to whom can they turn?

Yet Mountain Cove and communities like her cannot count on government help. Fisheries economists now contend that the traditional inshore fishery is uneconomical, and they argue that there is no point in developing more costly inshore facilities. But the only alternative to fishing for most Newfoundland communities is slow decline or sudden resettlement. The people of Poplar Point hope that the proposed federal park may rejuvenate their economy and make them an exception. But at the time we were there Mountain Cove has no such hope. Although the park may ultimately bring millions of dollars, thousands of tourists and hundreds of jobs to their area, the community was to be "removed".

"Where in the name of God are they going to shift them at?"

As their comments indicate, the people of Mountain Cove almost unanimously oppose the resettlement of their community. However like the residents of Small Harbour, they do not reject resettlement completely. They have observed the resettlement of two small nearby communities into Mountain Cove, and regard it as the right decision for those villages. They simply do not regard it as rational *for them.* Larger communities like Mountain Cove should be able to survive on their own.

> It's O.K. for little small outport places like that. But you take a place like this. . . .

Most argued that the resettlement of Mountain Cove was out of the question simply because there was nowhere nearby they could go. They vehemently opposed the suggestion that they might move to any of the nearby communities. Although these communities have a reputation throughout the area for hard work and a good standard of life, the

---

shallow river mouth, and only small boats can enter this at low tide. While some larger boats do operate from the community, they can only enter and leave port at peak tides and often have to stay out in dangerous weather because of this. Therefore most residents are content to use small outboard motor boats which they pull up on the beach. It is remarkable that they get the catch they do with such equipment. It would seem reasonable for the government to provide adequate fishing facilities for a community of this size. They have certainly provided smaller communities with comparable facilities to those being requested.

people of Mountain Cove regard them as inferior places in which to make
a living.

> No sir-e-bob. That's what we don't [think that resettlement is
> a good idea]. Not now and not ever. At least we got a living here.
> We're a cent above a beggar, but take us where we can't get a job
> and what would we do. The first man that comes here and suggests
> it [resettlement] is going in the water. They talk of putting us in
> [a nearby fishing village]. Why they're starving like rats [there]
> now.

> In a place like this I say it's a bad idea. Because what is the
> government going to offer 700 people out of here, regard to work.
> If they got no work here, they got none in Newfoundland. It
> wouldn't be nice.

> Not for us and not for Mountain Cove as a matter of fact. What
> are the people going to do when they leave. If they have any
> part of Bonne Bay in mind, it's out of the question.

Even the two respondents who favoured resettlement qualified their
approval. They felt that assistance should be given only to those persons
who wanted to resettle and only "providing there was a job to go with it".

Those interviewed were unanimous in their belief that the majority of
Mountain Cove residents were against moving, although a few did con-
cede that "no doubt there's a scattered person might like it". They felt
that older people in particular would oppose resettlement, and frequently
stated that most residents "got too much around them to consider
moving".

> On account people have their own home here, their own land
> here and their own fishing gear. You might say they have their
> own living here.

> Not many would be for moving I don't guess. And some, you
> would have to drag 'em.

It was only after considerable questioning that six persons admitted that
they had *ever* considered moving; two suggested that they might do so if
they were younger; and one person admitted that he had moved, but was
unable to get a job and had returned home.

The residents' comments were particularly interesting in the light of
the threat of extinction which hung over the community. Since they
vehemently denied any wish to move, one would expect that they would
resist the threat to their way of life. There was certainly no doubt that
they knew of the decision to remove the community: the government's

white paper had been widely circulated in the area and many had even read it.

> We had a book the [this] year about it; the Bonne Bay Park. Mountain Cove resettled by 1978 or 1979. . . .

> There were rumors going around that the government was going to shift us out, but I never heard nothing definite.

> It come over the news that the people would have to leave Mountain Cove. They'd have to lug me out of it on their back.

> I heard they would shift them to Bonne Bay.

> It come over the radio two or three times about shifting the people here and down in Sally's Cove.

> The one thing I seen about resettlement is the book Joey [Smallwood] had out about the park.

These announcements appear to have produced a considerable flurry of concern in the community, and some of the proposals obviously had become embellished in ensuing discussions.

> They say that if the park comes through here, this will be a place for camping sites.

> I've read that here and down the coast are supposed to be reserved as old-time fishing settlements.

One of the community leaders had even been approached by both federal and provincial government officials who were trying to sound out the extent of his (and other's) opposition to the proposed removal.

> I had two men here, one from the federal and one from the provincial [government]. And they came in talking about the place and wondered about moving it out. "Yes," I said, "there is people who would like to move provided they'd get a job of work." He said, "If we build a house for you in Stephenville like you have here, would you move?" I said, "Not if it was a golden house would I move to Stephenville."

All such activity and talk had long since died down by the time we talked to residents. One or two emphatically condemned the park proposal when challenged,

> The park is no good for we people. I'm a fisherman. When I can't fish I cuts logs. How am I going to do that with the park here.

but most were almost unconcerned about their future.

> People I don't think are too worried about it.

> People aren't concerned because I don't think they are going
> to resettle anywhere but the cemetery.

> I heard sketches of it this spring that they was going to close
> it down and shift the people out. . . . I haven't heard talk of
> it since the spring.

> We heard a bit on the news of shifting people from Mountain
> Cove. But we didn't give no heed to it. I don't see why they
> would.

Both community leaders and ordinary citizens appeared convinced that
such a fate could never happen to them.

Their comments suggested that the people refused to accept the
possibility of resettlement simply because it made no sense to them.
They could see no purpose in phasing out what they considered to be
a viable fishing community and no place where they could be moved.
By urban standards a community of 700 people may seem small, but
Mountain Cove was one of the largest communities in the area. Even if
the residents were dispersed among all the communities in the region, it
would be impossible for most to find full-time work. Some might be
employed in constructing park facilities, but it is doubtful that these
jobs would last once the park opened since residents lacked the necessary
social and educational skills. Above all they believed that free men have
a right to live in the communities where they and their families have
managed to survive for generations, and that no one has the right to
order them to move. This collective sentiment was summed up by the
man who declared:

> Where in the name of God are they going to shift them at? They
> can't come and force 700 people away. To force 700 people out
> of Mountain Cove is a big thing to talk about. They got to have
> someone to catch the fish and this is a good fishing port.

This ostrich-like posture might have left the community exposed and
vulnerable, but in this case it seems to have worked. On October 31,
1970, a "Memorandum of Agreement" was signed by the federal and
provincial ministers charged with planning the park. According to this
document "the area surrounding" Mountain Cove was to be "excluded
from the proposed national park . . . to ensure minimal social distur-
bance". Mountain Cove had won the battle it had refused to join. It
was allowed to exist.[12]

---

[12]The same was not true for the other communities threatened with resettlement.
   They were not mentioned in this memorandum and were forced to wage three

Commentary

In general this study focuses on the way in which small communities confront the process of social change. In particular it examines how threatened communities fight against their own extinction. I chose to examine Mountain Cove primarily because it had been threatened with extinction. I fully expected that there would be considerable reaction as the residents attempted to deal with this direct threat to their existence as a community. I expected to find the community reeling under the shock of impending doom, and its inhabitants desperately attempting to combat the threat. Instead I found that the people of Mountain Cove were almost unconcerned about their future. They did not see the threat as real and treated the government's announcement with disbelief.

The preceding analysis of Mountain Cove provides rich insight into the qualities which make a community *viable in the eyes of its inhabitants*. The basic reason why the people of Mountain Cove did not feel threatened by the government's resettlement announcement was that they believed in the economic viability and social vitality of their community. They were particularly proud of its economic viability. Ironically Mountain Cove probably was slated for removal primarily because government officials were convinced that it was not economically viable.

While my analysis of Small Harbour led me to question and expand the framework for determining the *social vitality* of a community, my analysis of Mountain Cove leads me to question the criteria whereby the *economic viability* of rural life is judged.

The basic measure for determining the economic viability of any economic action is cost-benefit analysis. This is simply a method whereby all discernible economic expenditures are weighed against economic benefits. If a programme or policy produces more economic gain than it costs to provide it, it is usually considered successful.

Cost-benefit analysis of this sort is often applied to government programmes and policies, but it can also be used to judge communities. For example, the federal and provincial governments undertook a cost-benefit analysis of the resettlement programme soon after it was inaugurated.

---

years of active public protest before the government agreed to even partially modify their stand. Even then they did not get full exemption from government control. In some, the residents were allowed to remain in their homes and bequeath them to their next of kin, who in turn could do the same. But their homes and land could be sold only to the government. Other communities were not so lucky and have already been "removed".

They were interested in discovering if this programme generated more income than it cost to operate. In order to assess the economic advantages of the resettlement programme the government had to determine whether it cost more to service the people of the resettled communities before or after they were moved. This required an assessment of all government inputs into each community both before and after resettlement and an assessment of the income generated by the people of the community both before and after moving. Thus the resettled communities themselves, not the resettlement programme, came to be judged in terms of their cost-benefit potential.

As we shall discuss in Chapter VI, much of the rural development planning in this country seems to take this form. It is particularly common among top-down developers who focus on the economic advantages to be gained through large industrial enterprises. In my opinion an accounting procedure of inputs and outputs is a questionable basis for judging a community. Even from a purely economic perspective, it is not satisfactory when applied to rural communities. Because of the subsistence nature of their economy, much of the "product" of rural communities is for home consumption and never enters the marketplace. In this sense the community is its own product. An input-output type of analysis is likely to underestimate the income generated by such communities.

In view of the considerations here it might make more sense to examine whether a community would require less government assistance if the people were situated elsewhere. However this is still likely to ignore the income generated by the community and lead to the conclusion that it is cheaper to have people move and end up on welfare assistance elsewhere, than provide hundreds of thousands of dollars worth of fishing improvements where they now reside. By this same logic one could argue that most of the provinces of Canada are uneconomical and should be resettled in southern Ontario. The most obvious flaw in such reasoning is that it measures only economic factors and ignores the social and psychological dimensions of community life. An analysis from a social or psychological perspective might well conclude that the social and psychological costs of moving people far exceed any economic benefits.

Even without a cost-benefit analysis, the government had considerable evidence for thinking that Mountain Cove was not economically viable. The high incidence of welfare payments made it appear that the community had disintegrated to such a degree that people no longer cared to work. Under such circumstances the government's desire to break up the community and disperse its population among those with more accepted value patterns is understandable.

But our analysis of Mountain Cove strongly indicates that the community is not full of dispirited and disoriented people who are unwilling to work. Undoubtedly some fit this description, but most work year round in a variety of primary jobs. They are absolutely convinced that their community is economically viable because of income derived from a variety of sources including fishing, mining, logging and farming. Some may consider the system of supplementing earned income with welfare assistance one of the reasons why Mountain Cove is economically viable, but I am inclined to believe the majority of respondents who maintained that few obtain such payments. In any case, their use of government assistance can be compared to the actions of the founders of Mountain Cove who continued to fish lobster in spite of government prohibition and harassment. Both are the rebellious acts of men struggling to exist under conditions of marginal subsistence. Rather like a guaranteed annual income, the government welfare payments make the difference between living below or above the poverty line.

Moral considerations aside, our analysis of Mountain Cove shows that there are varying criteria of economic viability. Formal techniques such as cost-benefit analysis are useful in examining the *objective* basis of a community's economic viability, but the residents may use more *subjective* criteria. These approaches are based on very different values. The objective approach is based on the goals of economic gain and profit maximization, while the subjective is based on "quality of life" considerations in addition to purely economic ones. In short, the perception of economic vitality is *socially* determined.

From their subjective perspective the people of Mountain Cove considered resettlement economically irrational. It would be impossible for them to "live as well" in any other nearby community. Moreover, they were making an economic contribution in Mountain Cove which would be impossible elsewhere. For them, Mountain Cove was the best place to make a living.

Perhaps it was the government's realization that it would be virtually impossible to find ways to support Mountain Cove's 700 people in nearby communities that led them to change their plans. The original park proposal quoted at the beginning of this chapter suggests that provincial authorities were aware of the problem from the beginning, but that the officials in Ottawa had to be convinced. This is understandable since the values of the urban centre are not always those of the rural fringe: it is unlikely that Ottawa's planners could see the world through the eyes of the people of Mountain Cove. Too often policy is high-handed simply because it is based on values which are different from those of the people it affects.[13]

Mountain Cove residents assess the economic viability of their community rather differently than do outsiders. From their perspective, based on their own values and goals, Mountain Cove is a highly viable place in which to live. Although they may be accused of being biased, I have tried to show how so-called "objective" assessments of community economic viability are also one-sided and biased. I believe that both types of analysis are necessary if we are to obtain a true perspective of a community's economic viability.

It would not do to conclude the discussion of Mountain Cove without some comment on its social vitality. The formal aspects of the community's social structure indicate that Mountain Cove has few, if any of the problems which plagued Small Harbour. Primarily because of its larger size, the community has its own modern schools including a large high school. It is linked by road to the outside world and, even at the height of winter, this road is rarely closed for more than a few hours at any time. Because of this easy accessibility, the community finds it relatively easy to attract qualified teachers to its schools and clergymen to its churches. The Salvation Army is the only denomination which stations (teaching) clergy in the community, but the United Church and Anglican ministers live only twelve miles away and visit the community regularly and frequently. The people's only complaint was that they had no resident doctor or nurse. However, except under severe weather conditions, it is possible for them to reach a nearby hospital in less than an

---

[13]The recently published case of the residents of the Gaspé Peninsula is an obvious example of an analogous situation involving both federal and provincial governments in the planning of a park. However the residents of that area were reportedly victimized by government and intimidated into moving in order to make way for the park (*Time Magazine,* July 14, 1975:9-10). In that instance Ottawa was in charge of developing the park, while the provincial government undertook the expropriation of property. Residents were offered "rock bottom prices", threatened with court action and with the loss of telephone service, electricity, snow removal and even the school bus if they resisted. *Time* indicates that government demolition teams even initiated midnight burnings of some houses. The absurdity is that a basic aim of the park was to provide jobs for the very people who were being harassed. The case of this park so closely parallels that of Bonne Bay that one cannot help but feel that the residents of Mountain Cove were extremely lucky. They would surely have been unprepared to resist such callous authoritarian action had it occurred in their area.

hour, and in this regard they are better served than most other Newfoundland centres of comparable size. The educational facilities, religious and medical services cause little concern among the residents of Mountain Cove, whereas they were the focus of concern in Small Harbour.

The only area of formal social organization which may be considered problematical is that of community leadership and government. The two traditional community leaders were the link between the community and the outside world and hold the position of leaders in the newly-formed community council. But the council itself does not seem to have been active in formulating a leadership role. The threat of resettlement would seem to be a matter of vital interest and concern to the elected leaders of the community, yet they did not respond to the government's announcement. Instead they directed all their energies towards administering the day-to-day activities of the community. Until it redefines its role, the community council is likely to continue to ignore the problems which threaten the future of Mountain Cove and make it the unresisting victim of outside planning and manipulation.

This analysis of community leadership opens up questions concerning the extent of community committment and co-operation. Their comments leave no doubt that the people of Mountain Cove are committed to their community: some live on marginal incomes rather than take jobs elsewhere. Normally, as we saw in Small Harbour, the committment of residents is the key factor which enables the community to remain socially vital even in the face of poor economic viability. Committment usually leads to a high degree of citizen involvement and co-operation in community affairs. But in Mountain Cove, despite strong friendship ties which exist between some people, there is considerable hostility and mistrust. This is a cause for concern because, without co-operation, there is little possibility of strong and unified community action.

Nonetheless there is absolutely no doubt that Mountain Cove is far more socially vital and economically viable than Small Harbour. The contrast demonstrates the variability which exists from community to community. Not all rural communities are the same: the ways in which they deal with essentially similar problems vary enormously. The community of Grande Terre is yet another example.

CHAPTER V

GRANDE TERRE

Early settlers came over from Brittany in France to fish around the western shores of Newfoundland. At first they used to return in the fall, a passage that took "about eleven days". Some of them began to settle and make their homes along the shores of the Port-au-Port peninsula. Up until seventy years ago there were families with their homes and their cattle on "L'Isle Rouge" (Red Island). Sometime in the early 1900s they moved to the "Grande Terre", the big land.

> —Booklet published to commemorate the opening of Our Lady of Lourdes elementary school, June 9, 1971.

"Early settlers came over from Brittany in France"

Unlike Small Harbour and Mountain Cove, Grande Terre was never given public notice that it was to be resettled. But even though the community has not experienced the same open pressure to move, it has been exposed to equally strong, if indirect pressures. Thus Grande Terre acts as a bridge between the communities previously discussed, whose existence has been openly threatened, and those hundreds of other communities who face even more subtle pressures.

Although Grande Terre was the last of the communities studied, I became aware of its relevance to my research at a very early stage. During my first "scouting trip" to the west coast of Newfoundland I heard rumors from community development workers that the residents of some of the communities on the Port-au-Port peninsula were unhappy and were talking of resettling. This was confirmed by both members of the Port-au-Port Regional Development Council and some of the local clergy.

In these conversations talk inevitably turned to Grande Terre which was cited as the community most likely to resettle. Reportedly the poor condition of the road leading into the community had virtually isolated the residents and had prompted them to consider moving. I was told that a month before a resident had become ill and the doctor had been unable to reach him because the road was impassable. According to one local priest, it was not until two weeks after the man died that the priest from Lourdes finally was able to get through to perform a Christian burial. Beyond these possibly apocryphal stories, there was little information available on Grande Terre or the Port-au-Port peninsula. Residents of Stephenville just fifteen miles away seemed almost totally uninformed about happenings in the area.

Perhaps this is because of the isolation of the peninsula. A triangle of land jutting some forty miles into the Gulf of St. Lawrence from Newfoundland's west coast, Port-au-Port is linked to other communities only by a winding road which deteriorates soon after it crosses the narrow isthmus. The communities on the peninsula are also isolated from one another because of the unusual terrain. Most of these villages are grouped along the south or west coasts, which are separated by high hills, making overland communication almost impossible. Because the road follows the contours of the land it does little to relieve the situation. Soon after it reaches the peninsula it divides into two branches; one travels straight along the south shore linking the communities there, the other angles northwest until it reaches Lourdes (1971 population: 903), the only large community on the peninsula. Grande Terre is some twelve to fifteen miles from Lourdes and is probably the most isolated community of any on the peninsula.

But it is not only geography which isolates Grande Terre and some of the other Port-au-Port communities. They are also isolated by ethnic and language differences. Grande Terre is one of only three or four French communities in Newfoundland, all of which are located at the end of the Port-au-Port peninsula roads. Few English-speaking Newfoundlanders ever visit these communities[1] but rumours about them abound. In early conversations with these "outsiders" I was told a variety of gratuitous stories about the pugnaciousness, lawlessness and proclivity for incestuous relationships of their residents. English Newfoundlanders even have a perjorative name, "jacquetar" (pronounced jack-a-tar), which they use to describe these Newfoundlanders of French background.[2]

[1] Many east coast Newfoundlanders are totally unaware that French speaking communities still exist on the island. Several have argued with me that there are none, while others have contended that any French population which once existed has now been totally assimilated.

[2] There is a common "myth" that these French Newfoundlanders are really not fully French but a combination of French and Micmac Indian. The term "jacquetar"

The origins of these people are unclear. The quote at the beginning of this chapter is one of the few published references available. It suggests that these people are descendants of French fishermen who fished off the Newfoundland coast. Others claim that at least some of the residents are the descendants of Acadian fishermen who migrated to the area from Cape Breton Island.

There is a similar lack of information on the social structure and culture of the region. Indeed, the French of Newfoundland are perhaps the only French-speaking people in Canada who have been neglected by social scientists. The only work by an anthropologist or sociologist is one brief article on inheritance patterns in the village of Cape Saint George (Lamarre, 1973: 142-153).

There is even debate over whether French is still the language most frequently used by the residents of these communities. A federal proposal to declare the area a "bilingual district" eligible for special federal assistance was met with a series of angry newspaper editorials and letters. The call to battle was begun by the St. John's *Evening Telegram* which argued that this proposal would "turn back the clock" and "create bigotry where there is none" (*Evening Telegram,* May 5, 1971). This was challenged in a strong reply by a professor of Linguistics at Memorial University, St. John's, who argued strenuously that the French language did exist on the Port-au-Port peninsula, and that those who spoke it were subject to discrimination. His views were based on his recent visit to the area. While he accepted that the older generation had often attempted to assimilate, he argued that:

> A significant part of the reason for their determination to have their children grow up speaking English was so that they could avoid the cruel stigma attached to being French-speaking, the slaps on the hand and the status of second class citizens, the insults and the name calling.

His views were in turn attacked by a resident of St. John's who claimed to have visited most of the communities on the Port-au-Port peninsula "thirty or more times". He argued that the French population in the area was not interested in biculturalism.

---

is often used to indicate people of mixed French-Indian parentage. While some Micmac Indians lived on the west coast of Newfoundland during the early nineteenth century, I know of no evidence to suggest that they intermarried with the French residents. Certainly the people of Grande Terre have no observable Indian features.

> The Jacquetar is a man with many excellent and commonly distinc-
> tive qualities and characteristics, but to attribute to him an awareness
> of, much less a missionary zeal for the cultivation of French bi-
> culturalism, calls for a unique imagination. (*Evening Telegram,* June 1,
> 1971)

He went so far as to suggest that most supposedly French residents of the
Port-au-Port area were actually not "pure blood Frenchmen", but the
descendants of inter-marriage between Micmac Indians and persons of
both French and Irish descent. He concluded that a careful enquiry would
show there were not enough "real French" to justify a bilingual district.

> I believe a census would show that if the jacquetar population of
> the Micmac-French, and the Micmac-English and Irish extraction
> be deducted from the pure French on our West Coast, the real
> French percentage would be shown to be below the required
> minimum for bi-lingual (sic) schools.

Presumably he believed that only "pure blood Frenchmen" were entitled
to receive education in their mother tongue. Throughout the ensuing
correspondence (*Evening Telegram,* June 1, 8 and 25, 1971), no French
speaking resident of the area ever took part in the debate.

"On the way home they had to take shelter. . . . And he went ashore and he ran away"

Grande Terre is probably the only French community on the Port-au-
Port peninsula whose origin is not completely in doubt, simply because
it is the newest. The French settlers in the area originally lived on Isle
Rouge, a large granite obelisk a mile off shore. At some time around the
turn of this century the people moved from this island and took up
residence along the adjacent shore, the *grande terre.*

The origins of the Isle Rouge residents are difficult to trace. The
French were given the exclusive right to fish Newfoundland's west coast
under the Treaty of Utrecht in 1713, but they were not given the right to
settle the coastline. Even if this had been granted, it is unlikely that they
would have done so for the French fishery was very different from that
of the English. Whereas the English preferred to "light salt" their cod and
dry it in the sun, the French cured their catch by a "heavy salt" process
in which the fish were simply kept in barrels in a heavy salt solution. The
British method required that much time be spent ashore drying fish: the
French needed to go ashore only when it was necessary to take on water
and provisions. They tended to establish communities only where it was

necessary to have supply depots, and favoured the French owned islands of St. Pierre and Miquelon for this purpose. Isle Rouge was, at best, a cache where these ships could take shelter from a storm, and where their crews could take on fresh water and whatever supplies might be stored there.

This is borne out by Thompson's documentation of the continuing negotiations between the French and English governments over the rights to fish and settle this coastline. In one of the rare published references to Isle Rouge he suggests that it and Codroy Island to the south were the only French depots in the area. As late as 1881 there were probably fewer than 120 Frenchmen living in both locations and virtually no others living on the whole west coast.

> The coast in question [Cape Ray to St. George's Bay] was not a fishing ground, except at Codroy Island. Even there only ten Frenchmen had fished in 1879 and decreasing numbers since [to 1881]; and between Cape Ray and Port-au-Choix, apart from Codroy and Red Islands, where on the last report there were one hundred and twenty Frenchmen, the strand was not used by France for fishing purposes. (Thompson, 1961: 49)

In 1893 there appears to have been a basic shift in the French government's strategy. Prior to that time most of their North Atlantic fishermen had been transported each year from France with only a small shore-based community operating out of St. Pierre. In 1893 the new French admiral for the area decided that the French claim could be strengthened through the strategic placement of shore-based fishermen from St. Pierre all along the west coast of Newfoundland. To again quote Thompson:

> The appointment of a French Admiral in 1893 as senior officer with a flying squadron to protect the Icelandic and Newfoundland fisheries foreshadowed a forceful French policy. One phase of this concerned the reoccupation of the treaty coast by the shore fishermen of St. Pierre, generally called "petits pêcheurs" .... St. Pierre fishermen who had traditionally visited Red and Tweed Islands were also to be stationed in ones and twos along the coast and picked up in the autumn with their catch, in the same manner as Newfoundlanders on Labrador. (Thompson, op cit: 151-152)

So began the migration of St. Pierre residents (St. Pierrais) to the west coast of Newfoundland.

Newfoundland census records indicate that settlement in the area is a relatively recent phenomenon. There is no record of any settlements until 1874 when there were twenty-nine persons living on Isle Rouge. By 1884 this population had fallen to ten, while records indicate that there were twenty-nine persons living in Grande Terre. The population of Grande Terre grew slowly and was only 149 in 1945. There was a dramatic increase to 332 in 1961, rising to 379 in 1966 and 402 in 1971. By this measure Grande Terre has not been a community in decline.

The historical data make it possible to pinpoint the approximate date of the founding of the community, but these facts are far less colourful than the descriptions of early life in Grande Terre given by some of the local residents. Many of the older adults are the children and grandchildren of the first permanent settlers. They have vivid memories of the stories of its early days as told them by their forebears.

Contrary to the belief of most English Newfoundlanders, the majority of residents insist that their fathers came neither directly from France nor from Acadian Cape Breton, but were fishermen from St. Pierre. If such is the case, they were probably the "petits pêcheurs" mentioned by Thompson. The oldest resident in the community can remember that old people, when he was a boy, often talked about the summer fishermen who lived in the area before there were permanent settlers.

> I heard the old people talking about "in Fervac's time" and "in Tierjean's time". Fervac and Tierjean come in the spring and went back in the fall. They were from St. Pierre.[3]

According to this respondent Fervac and Tierjean spent only the early part of the summer in the Isle Rouge-Grande Terre area and moved south to fish later on in the fall.

> They used to come here now in summer and fish, and to the Cape [Cape St. George] in the fall after the caplin had passed.

The first permanent settler in Grande Terre was a man named Pierre LaRue who apparently was born in France and migrated to St. Pierre before moving on to Newfoundland.

[3]Most of the interviews were done in English, although occasionally some parts of the conversations were in French. All of the quotes used in this chapter have been given in English even though parts of them may have originally been spoken in French. Because so little of the local history of this area has been recorded, I have chosen not to disguise the names of the earliest settlers to this area. In this way I hope that my work might be of benefit to future historians of the region. I should add that the person quoted here could neither read nor write in French and so was unable to give me an exact spelling of the names Fervac and Tierjean. I have chosen to spell them as they are here because I have been informed that people with surnames like this do reside in Brittany where most St. Pierrais trace their origins. However it is quite possible that these names were actually spelled very differently (e.g. Fervac'h and Terejean).

> The oldest [first] man in Grande Terre was old Pierre LaRue. He was
> my godfather. He was from France I think. He was the first here.
> The first head of cattle that came here was Pierre LaRue's.

This was recent enough that the oldest community resident, who was in
his early seventies, could still point out where LaRue had his hayfields
and grazed his cattle. LaRue was soon joined by Euvain LeCointre, another
fisherman from St. Pierre, who had been born in Saint Malo, France. He
had fished off Isle Rouge and chose not to return to St. Pierre. These
"founders" of the community were followed by a succession of other
settlers, most of whom were from St. Pierre, although there were one or
two Englishmen from the Codroy area.

Just why they chose to settle in the barren isolation of Newfoundland rather than return to the established settlement at St. Pierre is not
known. Some residents suggested that their forefathers had fled France
for St. Pierre to escape military service, and that the move to Grande
Terre was simply a continuation of that flight. Others may have been
press-ganged into the fishery and chose this means to escape. One respondent even remembered one of the old residents talking about such a
flight.

> He told me a story once that they used to go fishing in the Belle
> Isle Strait from the shore in the spring with a schooner. On the
> way home they had to take shelter one year from the worst
> wind . . . inside the bar [the sandbar at the northern tip of the
> Port-au-Port peninsula]. And he went ashore and he ran away.

We collected many stories about these early residents, but by far the
most colourful were those associated with two gentlemen named Cretien
and DuBois.

Pierre Cretien appeared on the scene soon after the arrival of Euvain
LeCointre. Rather than settle in Grande Terre he went to Isle Rouge and
was perhaps its first permanent resident. By all reports he was an accomplished fisherman.

> He had a lot of courage and was a good fisherman, le vieux
> Cretien. He had a lot of courage with the fish.

In time Cretien apparently grew to be the indisputed "owner" of Isle
Rouge. Indeed, according to local legend he made a fortune by selling
Isle Rouge to either the British or the Newfoundland government.

> Pierre Cretien made a fortune on Isle Rouge. The government
> gave him a fortune to make him go.

Why the British government wanted Isle Rouge and why they felt that they could own it by buying it from Cretien nobody could say, but many knew the details of the story.

Cretien reportedly took his money and his wife and moved to St. Pierre. But things did not go well for him there.

It's too old for me [before my time], but I know that he went away and his wife ruined him. She got hold of his money and ran away.

His money gone, Cretien returned to Isle Rouge. One or two residents can still remember how he attempted to re-establish there until the British came and forced him to move.

He sold Isle Rouge for so much money and he couldn't go back. He could fish there because that was in the book. It was written down that any fisherman could fish there. But he couldn't build up. Any man could fish.

Isle Rouge didn't belong to him. He was keeping a store [storehouse for fish] at Isle Rouge and started to build a big place on the cliff. And the law came and told him he wasn't allowed to do that.

Cretien ultimately moved to another community some twenty miles away.

The events leading up to the arrival of Captain Dubois are even more fascinating. DuBois, a harbour pilot at St. Pierre, was given money by a local resident to travel to Nova Scotia and buy a vessel on his behalf. Dubois purchased the vessel but, instead of returning to St. Pierre, he travelled up the coast and ultimately settled at Grande Terre.

The old DuBois was a pilot at St. Pierre. . . . He was smart, that old DuBois. He ran away with a vessel. When he was a pilot in St. Pierre he was given the money to buy a vessel, and he went off [to] Nova Scotia somewhere, I think, and he bought her. And she was a good one made with copper. I heard people talking about that. And he bought her in his own name. When he come to Port aux Basques he showed his papers and she was in his name and she come in [passed customs] as his. And he come to West Bay in her, he and his wife.

These stories suggest that Grande Terre and Isle Rouge were settled primarily by residents of St. Pierre, some of whom had actually been born in France. Life was extremely harsh for these early settlers. Many were probably runaways who could not afford to maintain contact with either St. Pierre or France and, because of language and cultural differences, had little communication with English settlers in the area. They were left almost totally to their own resources.

Many of those interviewed recalled the hardships they had experienced in their youth. In those days there were no stores in the community. According to census records, the first shop did not appear until 1911 and it had disappeared by 1935. The two or three small shops which are now in the community are all fairly new. Thus in the early years of the community those supplies which could not be made at home had to be brought in by small boat or carried overland from other communities. The condition of the paths linking the villages made this a harrowing experience.

> You had to walk to get to a store. There was nothing but a path.

> We was in woods and mud to our knees. [It was] a sheep's track.

One middle-aged woman gave this particularly vivid picture of the difficulties she had encountered only a few years ago:

> If we had to go to the store, we had to walk about six miles to [another community] before Mr. [merchant] started here. We had to carry a gallon of kerosene and tea wrapped in the same parcel all that way. It wasn't very nice.

> Women had to go in pairs overland to [a distant community] or Lourdes to get flour. They would carry a 100-pound sack between them. There was no 50-pound sacks in those days.

Such trips were not all that frequent for there was often little money to buy supplies.

> I was fourteen years old when I got my first suit of clothes. [It was] flour bags dyed.

> You know one time we couldn't get two cents for to post a letter. I see that myself.

> Then we had a piece of pork and bread in your pocket for a week.

> Fifteen years ago you couldn't get a pound of butter. If you didn't have it, you didn't have it.

> If you went to Stephenville once a year, that was a luxury. You were scared to death.

The situation with regard to housing was no better.

> Ten or fifteen years ago you just had a shell of a house. No power. Nothing at all.

> If you had bad wood, you'd freeze to death.

While most Newfoundlanders lived in poverty and privation, the people of Grande Terre lived on the edge of starvation and death.

For many years the only real contact between the community and the outside world was the priest. Then, as now, all of the residents of Grande Terre were Roman Catholic and the *Catholic Directory* for 1894 lists a station at Grande Terre. However the community has never had its own church and there has never been a resident priest. It was only after 1912, when the first priest was stationed permanently on the peninsula, that the community began to receive anything more than sporadic religious services. This man was of Acadian background from Prince Edward Island, and was fluent in both French and English. Since he left in 1928, all of the local parish priests have been of Irish background and it is unlikely that any of them could speak French.

Education was a luxury that no one in the community could afford. Although the census records indicate that there was a school in the community by 1921, several people explained that the teacher was sent out for only a few months each summer. Since this was the peak fishing period, many families were unwilling to let their sons and daughters waste their time with book learning.

When the first school was start I was too big. Big enough to help.

It was not until the early 1930s that the community got its first resident teacher and classes throughout the school year. One person explained how he was instrumental in obtaining a teacher:

Father O'Reilly [the local parish priest, 1928-1941] was priest down to Lourdes and we had no school [classes] here. We asked him the reason. He said there was no stove in the school. It's hard when a parish can't get not a stove in the school. We went to work, me and [another resident] , and we made a stove with [out of] a tank. It was a nice stove. So a couple of year after a teacher come up. She was keeping night school. She wanted the people to build a place on to the school for her to live in. And so in the winter we went to work to build a place just to have her. A year or two after that a young fellow [male teacher] come here. He's in St. George's now.

When a community cannot afford a stove for the school so that the residents can receive even the most rudimentary education, they are indeed poor. At least in contrast, Grande Terre today must be considered fairly well off.

"Around here they helps one another you know"

Today Grande Terre is a community of some fifty houses. Whereas Small Harbour is clustered around the sides of a picturesque harbour, and Mountain Cove (despite its appearance of poverty) is located in a setting of majestic beauty, Grande Terre is simply a string of houses spread out along some two miles of gravel road. There is no sense of focus or centre to the community, and one is inclined to reach the end of the road still expecting something more.

Grande Terre, unlike most Newfoundland communities, has neither a harbour nor a wharf. The community is located on a large grassy embankment about twenty feet above a straight rocky beach. All the boats must be pulled up on this shore each time they are used, for Isle Rouge is too far from the mainland to have any real protection from the Atlantic breakers which regularly storm the shore. At two or three places along the two miles of beach some fishermen have built slipways and erected a winch to help them haul up the larger boats.

Although it lacks a harbour, the community does have some ecological assets. Local fishermen explained that a major fishing ground lies within sight of shore and that this provides them with an advantage over those people from nearby communities who have better harbours, but lack easy access to fishing grounds. As one resident explained, "Fish don't live in harbours." The grassy plateau on which the community is located makes it possible for residents to cultivate vegetable gardens, although admittedly only a few did, and the hills behind the community are covered with a plentiful supply of small spruce which can be used for both lumber and firewood.

Grande Terre is devoid of any large buildings. Even the traditional merchant's premises (consisting of a large store, sheds and wharf) common to many rural Newfoundland communities are missing. The four small existing shops are either part of the merchant's house or in a small shed outside. The only privately owned building of any size in the community is a "dance hall" some 100 feet long which has been constructed recently by one of the storekeeprs. Several nights each week a local rock group performs there and attracts teenagers from miles around.

Not only does the community lack any major store, it also has no church. Indeed the community has never had a church. In the old days the priest would hold mass in the school during his visits. Now services are rarely held in the community. Instead a school bus operated by the parish is sent out each Sunday to carry Grande Terre residents to mass at the large church in Lourdes. The one public building in the community is the school. This one-room structure once serviced all grades, but in recent years it offers only grades one and two. The older children must travel by bus each day to attend school in Lourdes.

Before going to Grande Terre, I selected a sample of twenty-four households from the fifty-four on the post office lists for the community. These included a random sample of twenty persons chosen from the general population of the community and four merchants who were potential community leaders. I subsequently found that three of these respondents had moved from the community and two were away working, so my original sample was reduced to nineteen. I added one other person who, although not a merchant, was cited by several community members as an older and respected leader in community affairs, and an additional five household heads chosen at random from the list of general population. Thus the total sample interviewed was twenty-five households. I also talked to several government officials stationed in the nearby town of Stephenville and members of the clergy familiar with the area.

My first conversations with respondents soon settled any questions about their ability to speak French. Every male householder interviewed spoke English (although often with a heavy accent) and at least twenty also claimed to be fluent in French.[4] The remaining five men professed to have only a smattering of oral French, although two of them said that they could understand it when it was spoken by others. Three of these had English surnames and were probably descendants of the Englishmen from Codroy who had settled in the community. The other two were of French background and it seemed unusual that they had difficulty speaking French, especially since some of their siblings spoke the language fluently. Further probing indicated that they probably did speak French, but felt that they spoke it so poorly that they could not claim to be bilingual. As one of them explained, "The French here is all broke up anyway."

---

[4] I would add that, even though my own ability to speak and understand French is limited, I was able to formulate simple questions in French which these people could understand and I had little trouble following the conversations between my respondents and the members of their households. Only one person with whom we talked knew no English. This was an elderly woman whose husband translated most of our questions to her before they both agreed on an answer. These two residents provided most of the information concerning the founding of the community and its early settlers.

It is quite possible that the French language is dying out in Grande Terre. When asked if the people changed any during his lifetime, one man suggested that this was true.

> I'd say they've changed. You take forty years ago, 90 percent was French here. You take today, it's mostly half and half I'd say. There's more English now.

However many young people and children are still able to converse fluently in French. This was obvious from listening to the general chatter which went on in many households, for the interviews frequently took place in the kitchen with the whole family coming and going. In order to substantiate these observations all of the sample households were asked whether each person could speak, read and write French. Out of our sample of twenty-five households, nineteen had school-aged children living at home. In eleven of these households the children spoke French. But it would seem that the first language which children learned was English, since it was rare to find children under age four who could speak French even though their slightly older siblings could. When we asked why this was the case we were told "they're too young" to speak French yet.[5]

While almost every adult spoke French fluently, none of them was able to write the language and only two indicated any ability to "read it a little". From their comments it would appear that the community has never had a resident who was literate in French. This does not indicate that community members do not "know" French since the situation is the same with regard to English. Although every household head interviewed spoke English, twelve of them had never been to school and only five had completed grade five. Not one had finished high school. The large majority of the sample was simply unable to read and write in either language. One informant explained that only two children from Grande Terre had completed high school (grade eleven) in the past sixteen years, and it is unlikely that any could have attended high school before that.

---

[5]Given these data we were surprised to hear the local parish priest claim that the children of Grande Terre no longer spoke French. As proof of this he cited the fact that many had failed French courses when they were transferred to the Lourdes high school. Further investigation suggested that there are several reasons which might lead him to believe this. First, he himself speaks little French. Second, the school at Lourdes primarily tests reading and writing ability in French and not oral ability. Third, there was some indication that the people of Grande Terre are hesitant to speak French in the presence of outside persons of authority.

However the education of these household heads was considerably better than it would have been had several not availed themselves of special assistance to attend adult education courses in Stephenville during the previous two or three years. Under this programme three respondents had completed grades seven or eight and another, grade ten. One had even used his new educational standing to enroll in a trades college. Like the residents of the two other communities studied, the people of Grande Terre use the allowance paid to them while they pursue their studies, to enable them to remain in their community. The one person in the sample who had graduated from trades college was unemployed and in receipt of welfare assistance. Because of his large family he contended that he was better off "on welfare" than working

> Not much gains in that. With the wages they're paying it's not enough for the shoes for a man with a family.

The average (mean) age of the household heads in the sample was 47.2 years, somewhat higher than in Mountain Cove and lower than in Small Harbour. There were fewer older people in the community than one might normally expect; only four (two men and two women) were older than sixty-fve at the time of the interviews. All but five of the men interviewed were born in the community and three others had moved there with their families at a very early age. The remaining two had moved into the community when they married.

As there are few French communities in Newfoundland, the possibilities for inter-marriages were limited. A higher than expected proportion of the wives (twelve out of twenty-two) were born in Grande Terre, while four others had moved to the community at an early age, thus raising the rate of endogamy even higher. The marriage and migration patterns of the sample are particularly interesting because they suggest that there is considerable interchange between Grande Terre and Cape St. George, eighty miles away by road and twelve miles away by sea. Both are undoubtedly the centres of French culture in Newfoundland. Six of the wives had been born "at the Cape"; three of these had moved to Grande Terre with their families in childhood, while the other three moved when they married. The most unique feature of the marriage pattern in Grande Terre is the age at which the adults had married. Our data suggest that many women were married as early as age fourteen and fifteen. One middle-aged woman actually claimed to have moved to the community upon being married when she was only twelve.

But what is life really like in Grande Terre today? One good indicator of the economic viability of the community is the employment pattern of the residents. Thirteen of the twenty-five household heads interviewed were unemployed: two of these were old age pensioners; one had returned from several months work as a lumberjack in Cape Breton; another had been unemployed since his adult education course had ended in the spring; and two were unemployed labourers whose work histories were filled with periods of employment interspersed with being "in the welfare line". The other seven persons were "disabled" and in receipt of various disabled persons allowances from government agencies. None of these disabled men could be considered old. One was forty and the rest ranged in age from fifty-three to sixty-four. They constituted most of the middle-aged segment of our sample.

Many had similar work histories. For a period of fifteen to twenty years they fished sporadically during the summer and worked in the lumber camps during the winter, then they had become ill. One had acute arthritis, three others had required bone operations and at least two had contracted tuberculosis. They appear to be the victims of hard work under severe conditions combined with inadequate medical care and poor nutrition during their youth. By the time they reached age fifty they were no longer fit to work. Indeed almost the entire "work force" in our sample was under age fifty, with only one over forty-eight.[6]

There is a definite pattern to our findings with regard to age and employment. The respondents in the sample fall into three categories: those who are aged, retired and receiving pensions; those who are in the fifty to seventy age group and who, with one exception, are disabled and receiving disabled persons allowance; and those who are under fifty and who, with one exception, are either presently employed or have been employed or in school during the previous six months.

Although it may seem complex, this analysis has very important implications for an assessment of the community's economic viability. The high proportion of unemployed household heads is not simply an indication of laziness, of a lack of work in the community or that the community members are apathetic and alienated. Almost all of those who can work are working. Those who are unemployed would likely be unemployed wherever they lived.

---

[6]This includes the four able-bodied men mentioned previously who were unemployed when we were there.

The twelve people in the sample who are employed have a variety of sources of income. Most combine fishing with some logging, some general labour work, rough carpentry and work on the road—in short, "most anything". Even the merchants have extra sources of income: one owns a "dance hall"; another has a small van which he operates as a bus to Lourdes; and a third has a beer agency operated by his wife. Two of these merchants also operate "saw mills" constructed from old car engines attached to large saw blades protruding through a table.

Grande Terre is the prototype of the traditional subsistence community. People are not so much "employed", as engaged in a variety of activities. Even when they may not have a job, they are probably building a house, cutting logs, helping out at the saw mill, setting a few vegetables or doing one of the myriad other things which have enabled people to survive before cash and governments.

The tradition of mutual help which exists in Grande Terre is stronger than that found in most rural communities. Several people had spent at least part of the day they were interviewed working with someone else to build a house, cut lumber or construct a dam. One person even claimed:

> You could go to anyone at all and he will come. They're good like that around here. Around here they helps one another you know.

Another added:

> Oh yes, just mention it and they'd be right there. Without [paying them] now you wouldn't have 'em for too many days. But just for a day, or two or three, no problems at all, no problems at all. You can almost judge that your own self.

Most remote Newfoundland communities still pride themselves on their neighbourliness, but in many co-operation without financial reimbursement has died out due to the availability of cash wages and welfare assistance. In Grande Terre this spirit seems very much alive.

> There's a man got a piece of land there this summer and he had two or three fellows there working for three or four days. And he didn't pay them because they told me. [They worked] just for to help the man out cause he was busy fishing, and those fellows here were living off of the welfare and they had nothing to do. So they got there and they put up that fence all around that land over there. They didn't charge nothing.

> Down there I'm putting a breakwater across that river, down there. I've got five or six men down there and they're not charging me.

And I'm sure that it's going to take me a week to do it. Now I don't
say that they're going to stand there with me the whole week.
They might have to go home and do a little thing for themselves.
But they're there helping me and they're not going to charge me.

These comments indicate that being unemployed or on welfare assistance in Grande Terre does not necessarily mean that one is not working.
Many of those people on welfare and even some who are technically
disabled freely help out their neighbours as the need arises. In a community as traditionally oriented as Grande Terre the distinction between
being employed and being unemployed is not clear cut.

But while the spirit of co-operation and mutual aid seems stronger
in Grande Terre than in most other communities, not everyone in the
community is part of it. Most sharing follows specific patterns usually
determined by kinship and age. For example, some storekeepers employed
their sons or sons-in-law (and even one or two other young men) as part-
time, unsalaried employees. For their labours the young men may receive
accommodation for themselves and their wives, food, building materials
and other types of assistance. Others helped their brothers.

It's what we're doing all the time. There's no shortage of them.
There's thirteen in all.

Similarly the aged people in the community received assistance from
their sons, and in return the sons might receive small gifts of cash from
the old age pensions. People with few family ties in the community and
those with poor reputations were likely to have little involvement in such
exchange relationships.

The people of Grande Terre undoubtedly live far better than in the
past, but they still do not live very well. The quality of their houses is
probably between that of Small Harbour and Mountain Cove. While
there are few large two-storey homes of the type common in Small Harbour, their houses appear to be more solid, in better repair and more recently painted than was the case in Mountain Cove. Most people live in
relatively small bungalows. If their housing is better than in some other
communities, it is not so much a sign of wealth as of industry, ingenuity
and co-operation. They cut the timber themselves, saw it into lumber in
the merchants' sawmills, perhaps in exchange for their help in other ways,
and build their own houses. Little cash is needed.

In short, Grande Terre is in some ways a "throw back" to the rural
Newfoundland way of life of a couple of generations ago. While government assistance, better facilities and ready cash have altered the com-

munity considerably in recent years, it is still the most traditional community I have encountered. Undoubtedly it has remained this way because it has been an isolated pocket of French culture in an overwhelmingly English society. The implications of Grande Terre's traditionalism for our analysis will become clearer as we proceed.

"I've always said that I would leave my bones here. Providing, that is, I'm not froze out"

Do the people of Grande Terre wish to remain where they are, and how stable is their community? One indication of both points is the rate of migration (including seasonal migration) from the community. Of the household heads interviewed, fifteen of the twenty-five had never lived anywhere else but Grande Terre, except for a few months each year spent "in the woods cutting logs". Few others had spent much time out of the community: four had been to Cape St. George "chasing women" and fishing for a brief period in their youth, but only one had stayed longer than a year; another had been born outside the community and moved into it at an early age; two others had lived in Corner Brook while either working in the mill for a couple of weeks or convalescing from tuberculosis; and another two had lived in Stephenville for several months. The only respondents who had been outside the community for any extended period were a man who had spent two years fighting in Europe during the First World War and a man who had worked in a Halifax fish plant for four years.

Not only were our respondents in Grande Terre the least travelled of any of the three communities, but a smaller proportion of their siblings lived away from home. They had a combined total of sixty-six brothers, of whom only sixteen lived elsewhere, while twenty-six of their forty-eight sisters resided outside the community.

A more relevant indicator of community stability is the migration pattern of the children. In Small Harbour most children left as soon as they were old enough to do so. In Mountain Cove this exodus was reduced somewhat, but there was still a sizeable migration of young people. In Grande Terre it may still be too early to tell whether the current generation of young people will leave. Although three of our household heads had no children, the other twenty-two had a grand total of 171. Fully ninety-nine of these were under eighteen and ninety-seven lived at home. Of those over eighteen, twenty-six sons lived in the community and nineteen lived away, and fourteen daughters still resided in the community, while thirteen lived elsewhere.[7]

The majority of daughters had moved upon marriage and had settled in nearby communities. The sons who had moved were likely to settle in nearby villages, to work in lumber camps in Cape Breton, to be miners in northern Manitoba or to work in Niagara Falls. Their choice of Niagara Falls is interesting. Several of our respondents' brothers and sons were employed as deckhands on excursion boats in Niagara Falls. These were almost perfect jobs since the men could spend their winters at home and also made use of their seamanship skills. From the evidence of this sample, the people of Grande Terre seem to want to remain in their home community. It is too early to determine whether this will be true of the younger generation.

The twenty-five household heads also professed a strong attachment to their community and its way of life. Twenty-two of them indicated that if they had a choice they would still choose to live in Grande Terre. The only exceptions were two men who would consider living in Stephenville or Halifax because there "might be more work there" and one of the community merchants who admitted that he would consider moving under some conditions.

> If I could sell out and get paid for what I have here, I would
> go. But its hard to know exactly where I would pick. I wouldn't
> go to Stephenville that's for sure. In Stephenville you've still got
> to go away for work so you might as well leave from Grande Terre.

But he admitted that it would be unlikely that he would ever move.

> Right now I'm so far back in age, in education, so I might as
> well stay with what I got here. . . . I've got a half decent home.

He also indicated that he had never disclosed these sentiments to anyone else.

> No, I've always said I would leave my bones here. Providing,
> that is, I'm not froze [forced] out.

The majority of respondents indicated that they liked Grande Terre mainly because they had easy access to fishing and were free from the constraints of urban life. Their comments echo those of the people of Mountain Cove.

---

[7] It is interesting that none of the present generation of young people is marrying as early as did many of the parents. Only one person under eighteen was married and many of those in their twenties were still single. It would seem that the normal age of marriage is now about twenty-two to twenty-five.

You're able to do anything here. You can put in vegetables and what you got is your own. It takes less money to live here than in town. I knows people who left from here and they haven't got a chair to sit on. A man like me, no learning, I wouldn't be much good in town.

I like it because of the clear air. And if you wants to have a fish all you got to do is go out and get it. There is no water problem. All the wood you wants is there. Everyone owns their own houses. If you wants to plant anything you can. Everyone got land. You can get herring, mackerel, lobster and cod fish.

It's hard to explain but you can go around. There's lots of places to go and the water is right long side. There's lots of fresh air and if you go in the city you are smothered. That's the way I feel about it anyway.

For me, you're left alone. You do whatever you want to do and you're left alone.

Whatever you've got is your own. It's a terrific place for kids. There are no worries about being on the roads. There are always yards to be in. I love the sea, that's another thing.

You didn't have to pay for nothing and it's a fine place to live.

The way I sees it if I wants a [cod] fish or a halibut, I can set a trawl and come ashore with it. I can make a dollar. I sees some people leave the place but they'll come back. We was born on fish and we lives on fish.

The people of Grande Terre seem to have everything most urbanites want. They have freedom to do as they wish. They own their own homes and have no worries about mortgages or debts. They have clean air, good water, free wood, plenty of land and fish. From their point of view it would not make sense for them to move to a larger town or city. Most are uneducated and probably "wouldn't be much good in town".

As a result they were inclined to be critical of nearby centres such as Lourdes and Stephenville. They could see little difference between their community and Lourdes and certainly no real advantage in moving there. Lourdes was invariably described as "about the same" as Grande Terre. "Lourdes is a place like here," one said, "there's a lot of fishermen."

Some recognized that Lourdes had facilities which were unavailable in Grande Terre, but this was not a sufficient enticement to make them want to move there. They were more inclined to point out that people from Lourdes had to come to the waters around Grande Terre and Isle Rouge in order to fish.

> The people in Lourdes have to come to Grande Terre to get a living. We don't have to go to Lourdes to make a living.

> Lourdes is about the same as here, but you can't do so much fishing at Lourdes.

Furthermore, while Grande Terre is solidly French, Lourdes has had a considerable influx of English-speaking Newfoundlanders from the south coast. It is essentially an English-speaking community and one respondent indicated that he and his children had been made to feel uncomfortable there.

> The school at Lourdes, it's too far from home. And besides that they calls the people from Grande Terre monsters. We're not monsters here. They was always good people here. The young fellow [son] cry when he got to go aboard the bus in the morning for Lourdes. .... They see a person from Grande Terre, they rather kill him than talk to him. The first he go down there they say, "He from Grande Terre." The first thing, "Monster from Grande Terre." I don't see nothing wrong with people from Grande Terre.

Stephenville presents Grande Terre residents with a dilemma. A town of several thousand people only eighty miles away, it had once been a service centre for the large American air base located there. When the base closed, the facilities were donated to the Canadian and Newfoundland governments which attempted to turn them into an industrial park. Most Grande Terre residents see the advantages in living there, including more facilities, cheaper stores and many more potential jobs. But they resist Stephenville because it is "too crowded" and because they feel certain that they would be unqualified for any jobs which might be available.

> They lives a bit better there. For regards to groceries they is a lot cheaper. And if they want to buy something it's right there.

> Them in Stephenville gets things cheaper than they do here I suppose.

> There's better chances to get a job in Stephenville. I don't like Stephenville. [It's] too crowded.

> Out here everyone owns his own home and he can grow his own vegetables. In Stephenville you have to rent a house and buy everything.

> With our cheque we could never make it there. It's all right for anyone with a steady job. But without work you're nowhere up there.

> If I'm disabled here and can't work to make a living, what can I do for work in Stephenville.

> People in Stephenville who are working live better. But people who don't work don't live as good as the people here.

> No better in Stephenville for me at least. If I was in Stephenville, I wouldn't own anything. Here what I have is mine. No taxes to pay. More freedom.

While they could see that Stephenville might be better for some people, they did not think it was better for them. One person summed up this sentiment with the classic statement, "Stephenville is all right to visit, but I wouldn't want to live there."

Most people in Grande Terre were convinced that their community was getting better. Only one respondent failed to indicate that he thought the place had improved in the last twenty years; he thought that things were about the same. Most stressed such improvements as "more homes, more families and better roads" and that people now had more money for "people were hungry before".

> Twenty years ago there were no roads here at all. Only since Joey [Smallwood] come in [was elected] have we got a bit of road.

> There's more houses, more money going around.

> Well, such as the road and the way of services. Today the trucks come and get your fish right to the door. And there's more stores in the place and so on.

No one saw the recent migration of some families as any indication of community decline.[8] As in other communities they tended to regard those who had left as drains on the community and thought Grande Terre was better off without them. Several expressed the belief that "they'll be back".

If Small Harbour and Mountain Cove are any indication, the ambivalent attitude of many rural people toward their home communities only really becomes apparent when they begin to think of the future of their children. Although the community may be the "best place for them", many still encourage their children to leave. This was particularly the case in Small Harbour and less so in Mountain Cove. The people of Grande Terre fall somewhere between the two: fifteen persons argued that children should leave the community after finishing school; seven argued that they

[8]How these people came to leave will be described in the following section of this chapter.

should stay; and three were undecided. As in Small Harbour and Mountain Cove, those who felt that children should leave argued that there was little work for them if they remained.

> I don't think that they could make a very good living here.

> They got to go somewhere else. There's nothing to do around here.

> They should get out and make a better living for themselves, yes. There's nothing but the old people stayed here because they got to stay. I'd rather see them somewhere else and making a better living so that they could do better for their family than what we did.

Others had negative feelings towards the fishery.

> Clear of the fish, there's not much going on in Grande Terre.

> I think they have to go away unless they want to fish. A boy may not want to fish. But when he settles down they usually come back.

Those who favoured the young people staying in the community were inclined to point out Grande Terre's proximity to fishing grounds and the potential that existed to make a living from a variety of sources.

> If they're not too lazy to work, there's enough for them to make a living. A man what can't make his living at Grande Terre, he won't make a living nowhere else.

Some people thought that the best strategy was for the young people to work elsewhere for a while before settling in Grande Terre.

> When I was young I went away and found work and after four years I come back and stay here. So I must have been contented here, eh? And I believe any young fellow who would make up his mind to stay and make a living could easily make a living just as good as anywhere.

> They should stay here and keep up the place. Maybe go away for a while to get some money and then come back again.

When it came to their own children, both those who felt their children should leave and those who felt they should stay preferred this option.

The disadvantages of living in Grande Terre were revealed when residents were asked what they liked least about living there. One of their major concerns was the total lack of telephone connections. Until a year earlier the community had been connected to the outside world by the wireless telephone in the local post office. But since then the post office had been closed and the community was left without telecommunication to the outside world.

> What they needs here is phones. If you wanted the doctor or priest in a hurry, you can't get it. Before there was a phone in the post office, but they took the office away. I got nothing to say about the mail. We can get it at the door. But my God yes, the phone would be a good thing.

> The only thing I feel should be around is the phones. To find out anything you have to go to Lourdes. Clear of that I don't see any difference from anywhere else.

> You see we got no phones. If you want to talk over the phone, you got to go all the way down to Lourdes.

But the major aggravation was the poor condition of the roads. The road to Lourdes was little more than topsoil and loose gravel laid over muskeg. During spring runoff it was impassable.

> We should have better roads than what we got there now. Joey Smallwood promised us long enough. And telephones we never had yet.

> I don't like the roads. Also its an awfully wet place. There's a lot of bogs.

> The only bit we got to complain about is the roads. They could be better than that.

> The one thing I'd like is a good road. This is only a one way [narrow] road.

> Well one thing I don't like, we haven't got the good road like we should. And no telephone. Besides that there's not much.

> The roads. I like living here but we don't have anything. It's the same as in my father's time.

The roads were so bad that three months before the whole community had hovered on the brink of evacuation. Many people had come to the conclusion that they had no other choice but to go. Several families had even left, taking advantage of new resettlement regulations which allowed the government to move individual families rather than entire communities.

How the community nearly came to resettle is a tale of pressure and covert intimidation. How they came to organize and overcome these pressures is an example of community resistance which places Grande Terre in the same category as Small Harbour and Mountain Cove. In order to understand how this situation developed it is necessary to first examine the nature of leadership in Grande Terre.

"There's nobody to speak up or call a meeting"

As we have seen in previous chapters, the pattern of leadership in a community is critically important in determining how it handles the pressures and forces of change. Both Small Harbour and Mountain Cove had strong patterns of traditional leadership as well as newly-elected community councils. In the old days Grande Terre also had leaders who ordered community life. Indeed there was no other authority to whom community members could turn, for they were cut off from the outside world. In those days:

> Old John Moores was the boss of the place. If they had any
> trouble with their land they would get John Moores. He
> would put your picket and say, "make your fence there", and
> that was all of it. There's no one like that now.

But in recent years Grande Terre has lacked a strong community leader. No local person has had sufficient power, authority or charisma to either link the community together or act as its spokesman to the outside world. And no one has taken any initiative in attempting to organize a community council. [9]

The lack of leadership became obvious when respondents were asked to name the leaders of their community. Usually a stunned silence was followed by such statements as: "There's nobody like that," "I don't know who it could be" and "There's nobody does it." One person even realized that this was the root of many community difficulties.

> That's the reason now today that this and that is not done.
> There's no people like that. There's nobody to speak up or
> call a meeting.

And in an ironic contrast with conditions in the past, one younger respondent claimed, "If there's a dispute over land, they fight it out." Only one person residing in the community was cited as a community leader by more than three people. He was an older man who was well liked and respected for his contribution to the school and the church. But he had never taken on the dual tasks of integrator and spokesman which signify a true community leader.

[9]Since we collected our data the community has formed a community council.

There are several probable reasons for the lack of leadership. No stores in the community are large enough to produce a merchant who is sufficiently rich and powerful to dominate community life. The four stores that do exist are small and tend to serve only the neighbouring homes and members of the proprietor's extended family. The competition between stores prevents any one person from taking precedence. Furthermore the merchants lack the necessary education to become community leaders; none of them had been to school, and at least three of the four could not read and write. It would be virtually impossible for them to take on the job of petitioning outside agencies for community services.

The people of Grande Terre most frequently named as their community leaders two persons who were not even residents—the parish priest and the schoolteacher for the primary school. The priest, who was stationed at Lourdes and rarely visited the community, was mentioned by four residents. The schoolteacher, a daughter of one of the community residents, had married a man from Lourdes and, although widowed, still maintained her home there. She received the overwhelming praise of sixteen out of twenty-five respondents.

The position of the priest in the affairs of Grande Terre is best described as anomolous. There can be no doubt that the people looked to him for leadership. When asked who was the community leader, one merchant replied:

> There's no one does it. . . . Because they don't know enough I suppose. That's the only thing I sees. They don't know enough. We got to go to the priest. Well now we thinks our priest, he's supposed to know a lot more than us and that's what we'll do you know. [We'll] go and find a priest. . . . When [the schoolteacher] is in the place, she keeps school up here, if we got a little problem we might go to her. But [for] a real big problem, well, we'd rather go and find the priest.

They found this hard to reconcile with the fact that their priest visited the community only in times of sickness, death or other emergency and rarely held services in the community. Most estimated that he visited the community "every three months". While one described him as "a wonderful man" and another pointed out that "he doesn't [come] very often because everyone goes down [to Lourdes] to the church", others tended to be more critical. The comments of one or two echoed the criticism which the people of Small Harbour made of their United Church minister—that he was only interested in making money.

Not too God damn often. The first when he come here he
was often up here. They come up here to get [to be]
millionaires. Then they take off.

Not very often he comes. When the priest come to Lourdes he
said, "I'll be up to Grande Terre once a month." He haven't
got much money when he says that. Now that he's got lots of
money he don't come at all. They're all working for money.

The rest used to come but he don't. It's too far. And when
the gas went up [in price] it's worse again.

[He comes] every three months when his car goes good or when
he thinks about it.

The priest, on the other hand, explained that this was a deliberate
policy. Rather than hold services in the small school in Grande Terre
where there was insufficient room, the church was attempting to encourage people to attend Sunday mass in Lourdes by providing free bus service. He claimed that it was difficult for the people to adjust because
in the past mass had been held in Grande Terre on other days of the week.

He was not optimistic about the future of Grande Terre. He argued
that one only had to look at what the people had around them to see
that there was really no future in the place. He was critical of the residents for not having taken advantage of the opportunity to earn good
cash wages at the now defunct American base at Stephenville, while bus-
loads of people from Lourdes had traveled to work on the base each day.
Nevertheless he explained that it was his policy to do whatever the people
might ask him to do. If the people of Grande Terre asked him to assist
them to remain in their community, he would do whatever he could to
help them.

If the people of Grande Terre were ambivalent towards the priest, they
were effusive in their praise of their schoolteacher. Although it is rare to
find a woman leader in rural Newfoundland, this particular woman came
by her position naturally. First, she was the daughter of the older resident
whom three people had cited as a possible leader. Secondly, by their standards she was highly educated, being one of only two persons in the community to have completed highschool. She had also taken some courses
at university and, at the time we were there, was away studying French.
The residents of Grande Terre unanimously credited her with bringing
about the improvement of the roads and with bringing the problems of
the community to the attention of government leaders.

She was born here. She's the one who went to a lot of trouble
to get the roads fixed up.

> She's a teacher. . . . She worked a lot for to get the roads.
>
> She arranged for the meeting with [the provincial government representative], and she tried for the telephones and stuff like that.
>
> She helps a lot, but she's not from here, even though she spends more time here than to Lourdes. . . . She went to try to get [the elected representative] out to get something done to the roads.
>
> She's a smart woman. Without her they'd have no roads.
>
> She tried to get a road for us. Only for her we wouldn't have got anything done on the roads yet. I don't see nobody else. She's the only one helped us. Although her home is in Lourdes, she still tried for us here in Grande Terre. Yes, the best person for us, that's her.

But the efforts of this woman must be seen in the context of the other activities going on in the community. From this perspective it appears that she prevented the resettlement of Grande Terre almost singlehandedly.

"The few that moved had nothing. They moved for the money"

The pressure to resettle Grande Terre had been growing for some time. Two years before this study residents of nearby communities predicted that it was likely to resettle. This was confirmed by a high official in the provincial government who assured me that Grande Terre's petition to resettle was expected in "shortly". The impetus to resettle was provided by decline in services. The school was the first to go, and all children over grade two began to be bussed to Lourdes. No one doubted that educational opportunities were better there.

> Down in Lourdes I don't see why they wouldn't get an education. They got good teachers and they're right in the heart of the place where the priest is. If they don't learn, why there's something wrong with their heads.

It was far more difficult for residents to accept the decline in local church services: the easy bus ride did not compensate for the loss of the priest's regular visits.

The relocation of the school and the church simply meant inconveniences: the loss of the wireless was much more serious. Not only did it mean that one had to rush to Lourdes in time of emergency, but it was also the first sure sign of government withdrawal of services. Whenever the road was blocked during winter and early spring, the community was as isolated as at any time in its past. The deterioration of this road was the last straw. There was little doubt in the minds of local residents that the government was deliberately neglecting them. Rumors spread that all money originally slated for the road to Grande Terre was to be spent on improving the roads in Lourdes.

Yet it is unlikely that matters would have come to a head so quickly if the government had not changed its resettlement policy. A 1971 fed-eral-provincial agreement permitted the province to sponsor the moves of individual families instead of whole communities. As part of its new policy the provincial government stationed a corps of field representa-tives around the province, including one at Stephenville.

Undoubtedly some residents of Grande Terre heard of the new pro-gramme and applied for resettlement assistance. But many were shocked when large moving vans from Stephenville arrived to take away their neighbours. Most were quick to claim that the six or seven families who had resettled were no real loss to the community, and that those who had left were poor people who had been lured away with promises of easy money.

> The few that moved had nothing. They moved for the money.

> Then it got in some fellows' brains what didn't know the difference, and what have nothing to leave behind, that it suited them. They'd get a better home in Stephenville and they wouldn't have to get up so early and travel to Stephenville for the welfare.

> Mostly all that left from here are turned down [disabled] and get a cheque from the government. Regardless where they lives they're guaranteed that cheque every month.

> They moved to get the money. They could get a couple [or] three thousand dollars.

> They are all family men, but they didn't move for the sake of the children but the dollar. They see $3000 and they went crazy. Now they are worse than us.

> They moved out just to get the few thousand dollars that's all. That's the only reason.

> Them that are leaving are independent. They gets a government cheque [i.e. their living is not dependent on living in Grande Terre]. The biggest majority are moving for the money.

Half of our respondents made such comments. The rest simply claimed they "don't know why they left".

There was also considerable criticism of the activities of the govern-ment field representative. His job was simply to explain the programme to those who sought information and to assist those wanting to move.

But those who remained frequently accused him of encouraging the people to move and of spreading false reports suggesting that everyone wished to move.

> It's just because [he] come along and give them money and just bought them.

> [He] is the head man of all that. He comes here and talks to these fellows. Especially now fellows that got nothing, just a little house stuck here and no land and no property and nothing at all. Well, he'll get them out see.

> Well, they met up with [the field representative]. He started putting down this news, sending this one letters, saying he'd pay 'em.

> [He] told us lies. The people went there [to his office] and he simply got their names and sent them the money. [He] was going all over saying this one wants to shift [move], that one wants to shift. All the time it was lies.

One resident, who repeatedly assured us that he had never sought information about moving, actually claimed that this field representative appeared on his doorstep one night to ask whether his house was built in one piece or two. When told that it was in two sections, the government agent reportedly replied that it would be hard to move.

> He says, "Is that building you got there built in only one piece?" "No," I says, "Sir, she's built in two pieces." "Well," he says, "She's going to be hard to haul." I says, "Hard to haul? What do you mean by that?" "Well," he says, "You got to shift from Grande Terre."

He claimed that the government agent then asked him to sign what was presumably an intent to move.

> That was last year he stop here, eh. He was going to give me a paper. I told him to keep his paper. I said, "Keep your paper." It come in my mind to tell him where to put his paper, too, maybe. It come to my tongue. But I said to myself, it's almost too bad to tell him that I suppose.

If this did happen, it was quite possibly a case of mistaken identity. Most merchants and respected citizens of the community felt slighted that no resettlement official had contacted them. They felt that the officials deliberately chose to contact only those who were most malleable.

> [He] used to be around smouching here and there as far I could understand. Trying to persuade people to move according to what I heard. . . . It seemed like he knew where to go. I often went to the road when he pass up [drove through the community], thinking he might stop you know. But he wouldn't have anything to do with me.

With the departure of some families, rumors about the inevitable re-settlement of the whole community flourished.

> According to reports 90 percent of the people were moving. It's rumors, eh?

Their despondency at the resettlement of their neighbours was obvious from their comments.

> When the cry was that everybody had to leave, and there was going to be no road, and there was going to be no telephones, well there was a good many downhearted.

> Gee whiz Christ. That's the worse thing they ever tried to do in their life. I was going to shoot [the local resettlement official] even if they give me the money. For a couple of years I was off my head. One was telling another the money they was getting.

> To move people from their homes, it doesn't make people very happy.

> I was pretty discouraged. I thought the place was going to shift. They was shifting the long term assistance receivers first. So that meant I had to go first.

> God know I can't understand it. No sense. No sense.

> Well my son, I was just about gone. I couldn't have stayed up. Well, I give up building [my new house] cause I had it up in frame you know. It killed me stone dead. Everybody was going to shift out, and me, I had this house here all up in frame and rough board. I didn't know what to do, keep on going or not.

> No, no, no, no, no, no. No. No. No. No sir. No sir. I don't see no sense in that. No sense in that. No sense to it. No sense to it. And all Grande Terre will tell you that, what's left.

All of the elements that make resettlement a self-fulfilling prophecy were present. The rumors were there. The fear was there. The government was convinced that everyone was going to move and so saw little point in spending thousands of dollars to upgrade the road. The people themselves were convinced that everyone else was going and that, if they were not careful, they could be the only ones left behind. They saw the deterioration of the road as proof that the government intended to force them out. When "resettlement fever" reaches this stage there is almost nothing that can stop the process.

It was at this very point that the local schoolteacher entered the battle. Her first step was to go to every house in Grande Terre and in neighbouring Rocky Cove and ask each householder if they wished to move. In both communities she found only two families who wished to leave.

> [She] went around. She had two lists; who wanted to shift and who didn't want to shift. I think there was a couple of families wanted to shift then and all the rest didn't want to move.

Armed with these facts, she consulted the priest in Lourdes. He was in a difficult position. In spite of his personal feelings, he was confronted with considerable evidence that the people of Grande Terre (and the neighbouring community) wished to remain. Perhaps to ensure that there was no mistake, he called a public meeting in Grande Terre.

> Father come up here and had a meeting in the school. And he asked us what we intended to do. Move out or stay in the place.

Once assured of the community's sentiments, he informed the meeting that he had already been in touch with the local member of the provincial House of Assembly and that this man was willing to come and meet with the people.

This second meeting did not take place until nearly six months later. The provincial representative for the district was the main attraction and he lived up to his billing. He promised the people that, if they wished to stay, $70,000 would be spent during the next few months to upgrade the road from Lourdes to Grande Terre and that the community would have telephone service by the end of the year. Three months later the road was already under construction. Like the people of Small Harbour and Mountain Cove, the people of Grande Terre had won the right to stay in their community.

When I arrived in Grande Terre and began my study, the community was in a state of euphoria. For at least three years they had lived with uncertainty. They had heard rumors that their community was "slated to go" and that everyone intended to leave. The post office had closed and the wireless was removed. The roads continued to deteriorate amid rumors that funds normally granted to maintain them would be spent elsewhere. Several residents had already received assistance to resettle and few, if any, could distinguish between this new programme which allowed dissidents to go and former resettlement programmes which moved whole communities. Grande Terre appeared to be a community in decline.

> People were so fed up by the whole idea of resettlement that they didn't even bother to fix up their houses. Some of them

never even wanted to go out and fish.

But on the brink of extinction, their sentence had been commuted. Not only could they stay, but their community was about to receive the services it needed. Grande Terre emerged strengthened. The dissident elements, those who wanted to leave and who had caused bad feelings, had left. Those who remained had, perhaps for the first time, a sense of community integration, of identification, of purpose.

> The people are all working together now. That's why we got the roads. And she's [the community] got to come up [improve]. There's no way we'll let her go down.

To a man they assured me that there was no talk of anyone leaving now. On the contrary the talk in the community was that those who had left now wanted to return.

> The four families [that] are gone, they wants to be back. Their kids are all beating around here because they don't like it out there.

> There's a lot of them would like to be back. [One person who moved] told me himself the other day and he's only shift a couple of weeks yet.

> What shift from here are sorry they've gone. They even come back to Grande Terre to spend Christmas.

> They left because we had no road. They thought that Grande Terre was failed. Now that we got the road these people will come back.

To the people of Grande Terre, their future and that of their community had never looked brighter.

Commentary

We have now examined three communities which have managed to survive the threat of resettlement and evacuation. Instead of finding a common formula for survival, we have discovered that each chose a very different way to achieve its goal. Each community's solution reflects its unique social organization and history, as well as the particular character of the threat experienced.

Small Harbour was slowly declining as young people left to seek their fortunes elsewhere, and families departed in search of better schools and less isolation. The community was able to survive only because federal officials inadvertently admitted that the community was slated for re-settlement. Armed with this information, the leaders were able to organize and confront the government, demanding that they prove that this was not the case.

In Mountain Cove there was no such confrontation. To the local people it simply did not make sense to move a community as big and prosperous as theirs, and they simply ignored the threat. They had several factors in their favour: few people wished to leave; Mountain Cove was larger and had better services than most communities; and it was not declining. It was probably these factors which convinced the government to reconsider its decision.

Grande Terre seems to have adopted an intermediate strategy. It was essentially a community without formal organization. Thus the residents were not organized to oppose evacuation, but at the same time there was little organized pressure to move from within the community. Rather the pressure seems to have come from outside in the form of a new government programme to move individual households and as a consequence of the withdrawal of some services. The community was able to survive, not because it was organized in opposition to resettlement, but because one former resident took it upon herself to act on behalf of the people. They survived because this woman provided information which ended rumours of a mass exodus and confronted the government with fact. She collected data which were impossible to dispute, particularly after the priest held a meeting which confirmed her findings. As a result the government backed down and agreed to provide improved public services.

But how secure is the future of Grande Terre? Upon what basis do we assess its economic viability and social vitality? These questions are important because Grande Terre is the type of community that most planners would like to resettle. It is isolated at the end of a road, making communication difficult and costly. It has no school and its standard of education is abominably low even among the current generation of children. It has no harbour and no real fishing facilities and it is unlikely that either could be provided except at enormous cost.

As we have already indicated, it is impossible to assess the community's economic viability in conventional terms. Grande Terre is probably the nearest equivalent to a peasant subsistence society that can be found in North America: it is simply not part of the market society. It is likely that Grande Terre would continue almost unchanged, even if the whole economy of Newfoundland and Canada were to collapse. Its economic self-sufficiency contrasts with the economic dependence of communities such as Lourdes. Many Lourdes men used to travel to Stephenville to work at the American base. When the base closed, the bottom fell out of their world. Many were unemployed for long periods because they no longer had the equipment or the skills to enable them to return to fishing.

The economy of Grande Terre suffered no such disruption and life went on as usual. One cannot help but wonder which was the wiser group.

As demonstrated earlier, the people of Grande Terre are never really employed or unemployed in the usual sense despite the fact that many receive unemployment assistance and welfare. Whether they get such assistance or not, they still are engaged in a variety of work-related activities such as fishing, gardening, cutting wood, repairing the house and the like. If they are not doing these things for themselves, it is quite likely that they are busy doing them for their neighbours. In this regard Grande Terre is like many other Newfoundland communities today. Many Newfoundlanders long ago realized that it would be economically advantageous for them to quit low paying jobs after several months work and come home to do these tasks. Their own labour enables them to provide for most of their needs, and the cash they earn during the months of the year that they work away allows them to buy those necessities which they cannot make themselves and the luxuries which only money can buy. These include cars, television sets and the other costly appliances which now make their traditional way of life even easier. From this perspective their work pattern is extremely efficient.

In such a context welfare assistance takes on new meaning. In a market economy welfare payments usually are taken as proof of the recipient's inability to compete for jobs and there is an obvious stigma attached to being on welfare. In a peasant subsistence society welfare payments have a somewhat different function: they provide a guaranteed annual income supplement similar to that recently advocated by some politicians and scholars. People on welfare in the type of communities described still have some subsistence "income" and welfare payments simply supplement this by guaranteeing that each household receives a certain level of cash each year.

In all three communities studied there were still many people whose values are such that they regard being on welfare as a stigma and who would do anything to avoid it. At the same time there were residents (particularly in Mountain Cove and Grande Terre) who undoubtedly treated welfare as supplementary income in this way.

Since Grande Terre is the epitome of a subsistence society, it demonstrates best of the three communities the difference between objective and subjective criteria of economic viability. By formal objective criteria the community's future looks bleak. It is unlikely that the economy will ever rise above the subsistence level. To do so would require some type of "bottom-up" development which would help residents to increase their subsistence output and provide them with skills. But from their perspective, their way of life is the most viable and certainly the best one for them. Nowhere else are they likely to live as well and have so much freedom and control over their lives as in Grande Terre. There is nothing to be gained by moving.

If the economic picture of Grande Terre remains rather clouded, its social picture is much clearer. At the time we concluded our study, Grande Terre was socially one of the most vital communities in Newfoundland. At the formal institutional level residents still had to go to Lourdes to school and to church. But this was only an inconvenience and not something which would cause the dissolution of the community. In fact, most accepted that the larger school in Lourdes had provided positive advantages, although they were still concerned that the priest had too little involvement in their community. But it is at the informal level of social vitality that the community demonstrated its real strength. While Grande Terre did not have strong internal leaders, the schoolteacher who lived there part-time had come to be recognized by nearly everybody as a driving force in community affairs. Furthermore the traditional pattern of co-operation and mutual help was so strong that Grande Terre operated more like a commune than a community. As long as most people were willing to do their part, they probably did not need the strong central figures which other communities required.

There certainly can be no doubt of the people's committment to their community. All those who would divide it had been "paid" to leave. Those who remained were steadfast in their desire to stay and help build the community. Their sense of integration and community satisfaction was the highest of any of the communities discussed.

Grande Terre most readily justifies our claim that rural communities should be judged in other than formal/conventional economic terms. From an objective economic perspective its future seems extremely limited unless it gets the bottom-up assistance needed for local development. It is unfortunate that the government chose to send a resettlement expert rather than a development expert to the area. However its traditional basis of co-operation combined with a new sense of community involvement and committment are strong indicators of a renewed social vitality.

CHAPTER VI

CANADIAN REGIONAL DEVELOPMENT POLICY: A CRITIQUE AND AN ALTERNATIVE

The community research which has formed the core of this book was begun with two basic goals. First, I wanted to discover *why* the majority of residents in some rural Newfoundland communities resisted the pressure to resettle. My second goal was to discover *how* it was possible for some communities to resist direct pressure to move and to change, when other communities not so directly singled out had been caught in the vortex of urbanization.

But as the research on these communities was being done, indeed even as this book was being written, I began to realize that my research had implications which went beyond the situation in the three communities I was studying. As I listened to my respondents, thought about my conversations with developers and delved deeper into the literature on regional development in Canada, I became aware that my research was really concerned with the whole subject of the viability of rural life and of the right of rural people to assistance in creating a rural setting which would enable them to remain where they are, rather than be forced into urban centres. I became increasingly aware that many of those who develop rural development programmes judge rural life by very different criteria than do the people who live there. While developers tend to assess rural areas from economic perspectives, the residents themselves frequently emphasize social and cultural considerations. It was this awareness that led me to formulate the analytic distinction between economic viability and social vitality used throughout the community studies.

At the same time I began to take a stand. Like Prime Minister Pierre Elliott Trudeau who is quoted at the beginning of this book, I became convinced that all Canadians do have "a right to the good life, whatever the province or community [they] live in." I also became aware that in many cases it is the community planner and not the community member who has the greatest say in what constitutes the "good life". My contact with the people of Small Harbour, Mountain Cove and Grande Terre led me to think that the residents' own values should have the greatest influence in determining what the "good life" would be for them. Undoubtedly this value orientation has permeated much of my analysis. The issue of whether or not a sociological researcher should take such value stands is an important one. As I have argued elsewhere (Matthews, 1975b) it is my belief that, when it comes to policy research, the policy researcher should not only take a position, but should highlight the value oriented issues which his research raises.

Were I to stop at this point, those who read this work might well conclude that the happenings I have described were either peculiar to three small Newfoundland communities or, at most, were part of a unique programme of rural development found only in Newfoundland. To the contrary I would claim that the experience of Small Harbour, Mountain Cove and Grande Terre has its counterpart in every region and province of Canada. It is my strong belief that the programmes and policies used in Newfoundland are part of a long-standing strategy of development which is being used pervasively throughout Canada. I believe that the basic thrust of Canadian regional development has been directed towards phasing out rural areas and towards encouraging urbanization and industrialization.

These policies and programmes are not intrinsically harmful. Not all Canadians want to live in rural areas, nor would they likely be able to do so under the best of circumstances. The problem with such programmes is that they fail to take into account the wishes of those who do want to remain in rural areas, and that they use inadequate and *value biased* criteria in their assessment of the non-viability of much of rural life. It is a value bias to assess rural communities only in terms of their economic viability and to ignore the social structure, culture and values of the people which together constitute the social vitality of these communities.

Ironically those who argue that social planning programmes must consider both social and economic factors are often themselves accused of bias by the supposedly "objective" economics oriented planners. Frequently they are charged with identifying too fully with the subjects of their concern and of deliberately manipulating the evidence. Thus Copes has argued that the anthropologists and sociologists who have written about resettlement in Newfoundland have been "driven to rationalize arguments that will seek to conserve or restore the rural environment to which they have formed an emotional attachment" (Copes, 1972: 147). Yet surely indifference to the plight of those disadvantaged by social planning programmes does not indicate objectivity and value freedom, but a very real value stand.

There is yet another aspect to this dispute. When sociologists and anthropologists are pitched against economists in a debate over regional development policy they generally fare badly. Quite often they seem to be arguing for planning in terms of "irrational" social factors instead of "rational" economic considerations. This is a difficult charge to counter for our whole culture has come to accept economic motives as rational ones without realizing that they are simply another value position. Sociologists who stress social considerations are accused of being "pie-in-the-sky" dreamers, and are chastized for proposing solutions which are "not realistic" simply because they may be somewhat more economically costly.

To end this book before considering these issues would leave my task incomplete. While I have demonstrated that many rural Newfoundlanders have a unique outlook on the viability and vitality of their home communities, I have yet to demonstrate fully the extent to which this outlook differs from that of most planners. Secondly, I have castigated developers for being too economically oriented and unaware of social considerations, but I have yet to document that this is characteristic of much of Canadian regional development planning. Finally, while I have argued that the three community studies presented here have far-reaching implications for all Canadians, I have yet to demonstrate directly how this is the case. All of these require an in-depth analysis of the direction and value orientation of Canadian regional development policy in the past decades.

Canadian Directions in Regional Development

Canada has a long history of regional development programmes. One of the earliest dates from the 1930s when the Government of Canada passed the Prairie Farm Rehabilitation Act. This was an attempt both to revitalize western Canadian farmland after several successive years of crop failure brought on by excessive drought (Buckley and Tihanyi, 1967: ii), and to overcome some of the rural hardship and out-migration brought on by the world Depression of the 1930s. Over a decade later a similar programme was established for eastern Canada under the Maritime Marshland Rehabilitation Act. Both programmes focused on land use and were concerned with rehabilitating existing farm land and opening up new land for agricultural use. While neither programme was directly concerned with social development both had important social repercussions.

At a time when small prairie farms were being phased out by the on-slaught of mechanization, programmes such as these enabled small farm operators to stay in business and withstand the pressures to sell out and move to the cities. But from an economic viewpoint they simply served to keep alive otherwise economically non-viable farm units. Thus from the beginning Canada's regional rehabilitation programmes showed a con-flict between economic and social goals.

The next major effort at regional development illustrates the same confusion between economic and social goals. The Agricultural Rehabili-tation and Development Act (ARDA) was passed by the Government of Canada in 1961. Although far more ambitious than earlier acts, ARDA in its early stages continued in the same directions as that of previous programmes. It focused on "land use" projects designed to "salvage lands abandoned as agriculture retreated from marginal areas" (Ibid.: 18). Most of these were small scale projects and there is little sense of compre-hensive planning. But by the mid-1960s the ARDA programmes began to take a new direction. A co-ordinated farm consolidation and rehabili-tation programme was planned for rural Ontario (Ibid.: 21). This was followed in 1966 by the launching of comprehensive development pro-grammes in several areas of the country (Ibid.: 22). These were made possible by the passing of the Fund for Rural Economic Development (FRED) Act which provided an additional $300 million in federal funds for a comprehensive attack on regional disparity (Poetschke, 1971: 272).

This marked the turning point in Canadian rural and regional develop-ment policy. The FRED fund reflected the prevailing view of the 1950s and 1960s that backward areas needed economic assistance in order to reach the "take off point" for self-sustaining growth (Rostow, 1956, 1964). The FRED programmes were designed to shift attention away from agriculture "land acquisition, drainage and land development" to-ward "the broader field of industrial structure" (Brewis, 1969: 128). For the first time the emphasis "shifted decisively in the direction of educa-tion, training and the provision of employment in non-primary occupa-tions" (Ibid.: 128). The FRED programmes were conceptualized in terms of total and integrated social and economic planning. They were seen as long-range planning strategies between Ottawa and each of the provinces. No programmes would be formulated until a research phase had "isolated the main problems and potentials of [an] area" (Poetschke, 1971:273). This was to be followed by a programme development phase in which strategies of development would be worked out between the two levels of government. Only then would the implementation phase be begun.

This shift from purely rural development programmes to a focus on industrial development and employment in non-primary occupations received massive support from a study of Canadian regional development programmes published by the Economic Council of Canada in 1967 (Buckley & Tihanyi, 1967). It was highly critical of the land development strategy of ARDA and earlier acts.

> The farm assistance policies advanced by ARDA are remarkable for their tendency to evade the question of what might constitute an effective solution for marginal farm units. . . . ARDA farm programs are judged unlikely to have had any appreciable impact on the problem of low-income farming. (Ibid.: 16-17)

The report provided two alternatives for promoting per capita economic growth in any area. The first was assistance with "development projects", while the second, described as "labour force adjustment" and later simply as "adjustment", covered measures designed to encourage the movement of population out of underdeveloped areas (Ibid.: 17). Obviously "adjustment" was simply a euphemism for programmes aimed at rural depopulation. The authors of the report were strongly in favour of this latter alternative.

> In the long run, departures from the area of origin will tend to improve the local balance between labour and physical capital (including natural resources) in favour of the latter, making possible the attainment of higher productivity for the remaining labour force.

> Under the conditions prevailing in most parts of Canada, it is likely that a low-income rural area must rely heavily on downward adjustments in the size of its labour supply before significant increases in local productivity can be hoped for. (Ibid.: 17)

It appears that the authors considered "adjustment" the goal rather than rural "development". They regarded development projects as the result of local pressure and felt these projects might compromise important *economic* principles.

> ARDA cannot remain immune from the pressures to provide "development" of a locally tangible nature even if program planners themselves realize the strong need for "adjustment". This pressure can easily lead to situations in which economic principles are compromised and projects are accepted for ARDA financing even when they are economically unsatisfactory. (Ibid.: 19)

The value orientation of this study is clear. The goal was an increase in per capita economic growth—a goal which the authors felt could only be achieved when large numbers of people were moved from rural areas. Their solution to rural underdevelopment was increased urban development: their solution to low farm incomes was farm consolidation and the channelling of surplus farm labour into urban industrial occupations. If they were concerned about the social consequences of these policies, their concern likely was tempered by their faith that economic gains are sure to compensate for social loss. Perhaps their greatest worry was that local resistance to their proposed "adjustments" would "compromise" their economic principles. They felt that one of the few accomplishments of the ARDA programmes had been to wear down this resistance and "soften" the opposition to the programmes of out-migration.

> It is a major accomplishment of the program that it also helped
> to soften public attitudes toward genuine adjustments in the
> rural economy. (Ibid.: 19)

Their work reflects the type of development planning which considers social factors only when they present hinderances to economic goals.

The framework used in this study seems to have been uppermost in the minds of the developers of the FRED programme. Thus the research phase centered on a consideration of the alternative strategies of development and/or "adjustment".

> The objective of the research phase is to identify the main
> problems and potentials of the area and to settle on a broad
> strategy for adjustment and/or development (Poetschke, op.
> cit.: 273)

There can be little doubt that the planners took the advice of Buckley and Tihanyi to heart, for most of the programmes formulated under the FRED policy contained some attempt at population centralization (Ibid.: 274-280).

Though much time, energy and money was spent on formulating these comprehensive new strategies, few were ever implemented. In 1968 Canadian regional development moved from the economic to the political arena. As part of his campaign for leadership of the Liberal Party and the position of prime minister, Pierre Elliott Trudeau turned regional development into a national issue. He argued that regional disparity had the same devisive potential as the more publicized French-English cleavage (Phidd, 1974: 174) and promised that, if elected, he would make an effort to rectify regional economic differences. After his victory he undertook to make good on this promise by establishing in 1969 a new Department of Regional Economic Expansion (DREE). This new department has encouraged regional development in Canada through three interrelated programmes of industrial incentives, infrastructure assistance and social adjustment (Francis & Pillai, 1972: 46). All three activities take place primarily within "special areas" selected by the department in co-operation with the provinces (Ibid.: 54-55).

DREE focuses on industrial incentives as the key to regional development. It would appear that underlying this programme is the assumption that economic growth will not take place in underdeveloped areas unless industries are established there. Thus large financial "incentives" are offered to industries to encourage them to establish in slow growth areas. A second assumption seems to be that such areas require different types of industry from those which they once had. A considerable proportion of available funds has gone to industries which have never established previously in these hinterland areas.

This focus on industrialization is supplemented by a programme of assistance to "special areas" within each of the underdeveloped regions. Basic to this strategy is the belief that these selected centres can offer particular attractions to industry once "substantial improvements have been made to the infrastructure and social services currently available in them" (Ibid.: 54). Thus "selected urban centres" (Phidd, op. cit.: 179) have been given additional large sums "to provide the utilities and services that *industry requires*" as well as "adequate social capital facilities to meet the needs of the growing population" (Francis & Pillai, op. cit.: 55, emphasis mine).

The new emphasis on industrialization and urbanization is a complete change from early Canadian regional development. In its wake most of the FRED programmes and many ARDA projects were cancelled. While some ARDA programmes, particularly those of the self-help type, still exist as part of DREE's "social adjustment" activity, the focus of DREE planning is on the industrial development of selected centres. There is evidence that the department is beginning to realize that population resettlement is more likely to move unemployment from rural to urban areas than to solve problems of regional underdevelopment, for there is a new emphasis on manpower retraining. As one department report explains:

> An induced process of economic expansion has little likelihood
> of success so long as the capacity of the people to participate actively

in the process of economic growth and social change is limited by
reasons of inadequate education, lack of enterprise, and socio-
economic circumstances generally. (Ibid.: 73)

But here again the focus seems to be on training people for urban rather
than revitalized rural occupations.

This new thrust in regional planning strategy has not been without its
political and economic critics. The Liberal Party has been accused of re-
warding industries for their political support (Phidd, op. cit.: 185-88), and
DREE has been accused of paying industries to close down old plants
in industrialized areas and open new ones in underdeveloped areas, so
that there is no net gain in jobs. Both criticisms were incorporated into a
hard hitting attack by the socialist New Democratic Party which questioned the economic rationale for using public funds to develop private
industry (Lewis, 1972). Although I agree with some of these critics, my
own criticism rests on other grounds.

It is ironic that Canada's programmes for rural and regional development are built on strategies of urbanization and intensified industrialization when 50 percent of the population already lives in only fifteen
major centres. It would seem more logical for planners to investigate
alternative life-styles and to promote strategies that would move people
out of urban centres.

But little consideration seems to be given to ways of improving the
economic or social character of rural life. Writing about Canada's west,
Robertson has argued:

> Between 1945 and 1965, Canada's farm population was cut in
> half; it continues to shrink by 10,000 farms a year. The federal
> government expects that by the end of the century, two-thirds of
> Canada's farms will have vanished and those that are left will be
> corporations. (Robertson, 1973: 95-96)

Much the same future seems to be in store for the rural fishermen of
Canada's east coast. Newfoundland's resettlement policy was the only
programme of rural development and social adjustment discussed by
Francis and Pillai in their government sponsored review of DREE programmes.

This lack of concern may be attributed to the Canadian government's
acceptance of the "growth centre" approach to development (Perroux,
1955; Thomas, 1972). This planning theory is based on the assumption
that economic growth is propelled by centres or poles within a particular
"economic space". According to this theory certain propulsive industries

can have such an impact on the space around them that they can actually alter its structural features. When this theory is applied as a strategy of regional development the focus is on the establishing of large "master industries" in selected geographic centres. Because of their size these industries can benefit from the economics of scale (i.e. "agglomeration economics"). They are also expected to link together regional suppliers and extra-regional distributors and to spawn a network of related industries in their chosen centre, thus accelerating still further the overall process of development. The development of large industrial enterprises and selected urban centres is seen as the key to regional development.

The men responsible for Canada's current regional development policy have indicated that their approach to development is not "entirely" based on the growth centre theory.

> The "special area" concept, although it draws in part on the "growth point" idea, does not imply that these areas themselves are all growth points . . . with clearly delineated "growth areas" . . . nor does it imply that the general strategy of the federal development policy rests entirely on the growth point concept. (Francis & Pillai, op. cit.: 63)

But the frequent mention of growth centres in the Canadian development literature and the major shift in regional development policy from rural development to urbanization and industrialization, suggests that current policy is directly inspired by the growth centre approach. Furthermore in a recent review of the growth centre strategy of development, the Atlantic Provinces Economic Council (APEC), an organization of eastern Canadian industrialists and businessmen, actually called on the federal government to intensify its use of this approach in the Atlantic region (APEC, 1972). Quite possibly this group has a vested interest in increased government incentives to industry.

This brief description of Canada's development policies suggests that Newfoundland's resettlement programme is not just a local aberration, but part of a general planning strategy used widely throughout Canada. Like Small Harbour, Mountain Cove and Grande Terre, thousands of communities across the country are threatened with extinction. As long as the value orientation of planners is towards theories of economic growth that ignore social structure and culture, these communities will continue to have to deal with the debilitating effects of urbanization and industrialization.

A Plea for An Alternative

Some years ago I attended a lecture given by a leading authority on Canadian regional development. He suggested that there are two alternatives open to Canada's regional planners. They can continue to spread their money thinly, spending small amounts in communities which are unable to support indigenous economic development, or they can pour larger sums into centres of demonstrated economic potential. He left little doubt that he favoured the latter course, and I must admit that I was swayed by his reasoning.

Obviously it is pointless for planners to pour money into small communities unless they also provide programmes that train local people to make maximum use of these funds and development workers to assist residents in overcoming the unsettling effects of social change. From the planners' perspective it is much more effective to spend funds in centres which have shown that they have the potential to support local industry and which have persons already trained to use economic assistance.

It was not until much later that I became aware of the weaknesses of his plan. Far from eliminating regional disparity such a strategy for regional economic development would probably increase the regional disparities which exist in this country. Yet the current growth centre strategy of urbanization and industrialization sponsored by DREE appears to be firmly rooted in these assumptions.

One of the problems with pouring funds into established growth centres is that most of the money will go to industrialists rather than to improving the standard of living of the majority of the poor. Such assistance may only serve to strengthen the elite position and affluent lifestyles of local entrepreneurs, thereby increasing social class divisions which already exist in areas of regional disparity. The people and areas most in need of direct assistance are those least likely to receive it: the independent fishermen in isolated villages and the wage labourers in hinterland centres will still be poor.

Planners often argue that funding the development or expansion of industries will mean an increase in the number of jobs and with this, an increase in the standard of living. But while the three community studies in this book indicate that rural people are rarely totally unemployed, these people lack the education and technical skills to compete in industrialized urban job markets. Some may find jobs as labourers while they are young, but by the time they reach middle age they are essentially unemployable and their numbers serve only to swell the unemployment rolls. Moreover as long as a vast source of labour exists, the worker will be at the mercy of his employer: wages will remain low and job security, tenuous.

Another weakness in the planners' arguments for industrialization and urbanization becomes apparent when one examines the type of industries attracted by offers of incentives or assistance. Many industries locate in underdeveloped regions *because* wage levels are low and workers lack organization. Indeed, many have been forced out of more developed areas because their low profit margins make it impossible for them to pay high wages and still compete. When they first move into an area of regional disparity they provide jobs and are welcomed because of this. But their continued existence depends on their ability to pay lower salaries than those paid in other areas of the country. Consequently, if a large number of such industries move into underdeveloped regions, they will permanently institutionalize rather than alleviate regional disparity.

It is difficult for local governments to overcome this problem. If, in reponse to the demands of local labour organizations, they raise minimum wage to the level of other areas, the industry will be forced out, leaving hundreds jobless. Their only alternative is to continue to subsidize the industry while it raises wages. This turns the process of providing incentives to attract industries into a programme of permanent assistance. To conceal the extent of assistance, the government may use less direct means of funding such as subsidized electricity or tax concessions, but this does not alter the fact that government assistance is virtually permanent.

In short, a regional development strategy based on urbanization and industrialization may not only fail to break down regional social and economic barriers, but may actually create permanent divisions between rich and poor regions and between elite and worker classes within a region. Such a strategy may also create a "dual economy" within the underdeveloped region. A dual economy (see Chapter II) is created when the rural and urban segments of a society are totally separated. While the urban segment is market-oriented and industrial, the rural is virtually a peasant subsistence society. In most cases a dual economy fosters a dual society: the people who live in rural areas have very different values, goals and ways of living that those who live in urban areas.

Current urbanization and industrialization strategies seem to be based on the assumption that the modern sector of the region, concentrated in large urban centres, will ultimately expand until it encompasses the entire population. But even though a large portion of the rural population may be lured into urban areas in search of work, it is highly unlikely that all will be so incorporated. If development assistance is not provided for those who remain behind, they are likely to form a highly traditional, near peasant enclave within an essentially urban state.

Another basic assumption of growth centre planning is the belief that certain large propulsive industries can alter the very nature of the economic system of the region in which they are located. Propulsive industries currently receiving government subsidies share three common characteristics. First, they are built on a massive scale in order to produce goods cheap enough to overcome higher transportation costs. Unfortunately size cannot long provide a competitive advantage. As soon as a factory of similar size is built nearer the metropolitan markets it gains the advantage. Secondly, governments favour industries which do not utilize or depend on resources which exist in the area. Ostensibly these industries provide a whole new economic dimension for the region. In reality, the sole reason for an industry to locate in an area, if it does not plan to utilize existing resources, is the government's financial assistance. When this assistance is withdrawn, the industry is likely to leave, too. Finally, in order to overcome these difficulties planners tend to encourage industries which use highly sophisticated manufacturing techniques. But this technological advantage ultimately defeats the purpose for attracting the industry in the first place. The more sophisticated the technology, the fewer the employees needed and the higher the level of training required. Since few people in underdeveloped regions have the necessary skills, trained technicians must be brought in from outside the area. Local residents are employed solely at the construction stage or, at best, in lower level positions when the industry begins to operate.

Two examples from the Atlantic region suggest that propulsive industries do, in fact, generate rather than solve problems. During the last few years the Government of New Brunswick has attempted to encourage the development of metal fabricating industries. One highly publicized example was their investment in an automobile factory designed to produce an expensive sportscar and act as a propulsive industry for the area. This factory did not use the resource base of the region: parts for the automobile were purchased from Detroit and Ontario manufacturers, shipped to New Brunswick where the car was assembled and later shipped back for sale in urban centres in the United States. The only reason for locating the factory in New Brunswick was the government subsidy. Without this assistance, transportation costs alone would have doomed the endeavour. The plant stopped manufacturing when government subsidies were withdrawn.

A somewhat similar case is the oil refinery in Newfoundland. Since no oil wells are to be found in eastern Canada, oil had to be purchased in South America and the Middle East, refined and then shipped back to world markets. To overcome the disadvantage of high transportation costs, the refinery was built on a huge scale and deliberately designed in such a way that the by-products could be trapped and used by other petro-chemical companies which might later be attracted to the area. But because of its sophisticated technology, comparatively few Newfoundlanders were employed at the refinery. And since no other company was attracted to the area to use its by-products, these few jobs were the only ones generated. As a propulsive industry, the refinery was a failure and, at the time of this writing, it has gone into receivership. Although the reasons for this are still unclear, newspaper reports suggest that the high cost of transporting raw materials to the refinery was a factor in its demise.

Throughout the hinterlands of Canada similar industries are kept alive only through high levels of government assistance. Many have already collapsed, leaving the provinces with little more than embarrassing and costly white elephants. These supposedly propulsive industries have generated a large number of construction jobs for labourers. But if this is their only advantage, the provincial governments would have done better to use the labour force to build pyramids which would have made considerably more appealing tourist attractions than either defunct automobile plants or dormant refineries.

Most of the regional development issues discussed here have focused on economic considerations, but they also have social consequences. The planning authority quoted at the beginning of this section implied that the primary problem in current social and economic development programmes is the allocation of funds. His main concern seems to be that the limited amount of money is spread too thinly to be of use. But development is more than just spending money. It is a whole process of engineered social and economic change[1], and it must deal with the complex set of conditions which *together* produce regional poverty.

[1]Given the nature of the following discussion, it is useful to distinguish between

A considerable insight into these conditions is provided by Herbert Gans who argues that poverty remains, despite our attempts to eradicate it, because it is "functional" to large segments of our society (Gans, 1972). He demonstrates that the presence of poor people in a society means social, economic, political and cultural benefits for those who are in more favoured positions. Applying much the same argument to regional poverty, Ernest Mandel argues that western capitalist societies allow regional disparity because underdeveloped regions can be used to advantage by wealthier neighbouring regions. According to Mandel poor regions not only provide raw materials and markets which are required by richer ones, but they ensure a large body of floating labour which can be enlisted when times are good, and dismissed when depression approaches (Mandel, 1974). He goes so far as to argue that the capitalist economic system would be unable to function without regions of relative disparity.

Gans and Mandel try to discover ways of overcoming the problems of poverty and regional disparity respectively. Gans searches for alternative ways to fulfil the functions which poverty now fulfills, but reluctantly concludes that some functions cannot be performed in any other way. Like Gans, Mandel argues that regional poverty is endemic to the capitalist system. He contends that regional disparity can be overcome only in a socialist system aimed at equality rather than profit maximization.

> In contrast with new-capitalist 'programming', which wants to entice capitalists into investing where they do not normally have an interest in investing when motivated only by the imperatives of private profit and the laws of the market, socialist planning aims at balanced regional development as a priority, just as it aims at free health care and education on all levels, or the abolition of all material privileges and all important inequalities of wealth. For

_____

the processes of social change, modernization and social and economic development. As I use the terms, *social and economic change* are the "natural" processes which occur at all times and in all societies, although the rate of change varies enormously from one sphere to another and from one time period to another in any society. *Modernization* refers to the combined process of social and economic change in a society which moves from a traditional social and economic structure to a more modern one. Although the term usually implies industrialization, urbanization and rational bureaucratization, societies vary considerably in the extent to which they incorporate both traditional and modern features into their social structure and economy. Thus it is possible for a society to become essentially modern while maintaining a traditional craft economy diversified throughout smaller towns and villages. Switzerland seems to be a case in point. *Social and economic development* differs from social and economic change and modernization in that it is not "natural" but entails the whole process of planning and engineering designed to alter the social structure and economy of a society.

all these conditions are absolutely necessary in order to achieve the conditions of social equality—equality of individual opportunity—without which socialism would remain only a premise. (Mandel, 1974: 12)

Although his belief that capitalist economic principals foster regional disparity is both well-reasoned and well-documented, this conclusion seems to be more a statement of ideological belief than a logical consequence of his previous argument.

Nevertheless the works of Gans and Mandel do serve to demonstrate the complexity of the problem. Gans essentially concludes that poverty must persist because there is no alternative to it within the capitalist system. But he never questions the system. In contrast Mandel argues that the solution to regional poverty can be found only in a system which makes the welfare of the population, rather than profit maximization its central goal. Both Gans' and Mandel's works make it clear that simply providing money and services to selected growth centres is unlikely to bring about the changes desired. In fact such a strategy may produce just the opposite effect by maintaining the existing status quo so that far-reaching change is impossible.

But is there an alternative? Fundamental change in Canada's economic and class structure may be needed but this solution seems a utopian dream. Planners and politicians are not likely to advocate such changes, and there is no evidence to suggest that the people of underdeveloped regions will demand that they do so. A more realistic alternative must begin with developing a body of practical suggestions and guidelines for changing the direction of current regional development policy.

The fundamental problem with a great deal of present development planning is that it sees industrialization and urbanization as the only alternative open to underdeveloped regions. Planners maintain that a region must choose between remaining backward and stagnant or embracing all aspects of modernity. When it is expressed in these terms, industrialization and urbanization seem the only logical choice.

But the preceding community studies show that there is a distinct difference between the values of the planners and those for whom they plan. The people of Small Harbour, Mountain Cove and Grande Terre do not consider their communities stagnant or backward. They see their communities as viable places in which to live and work, and choose not to move to larger industrial centres.

In the commentaries on the communities I argued for a strategy of development which would be based on the values of the people affected and which would maintain the way of life they prefer. This argument is based on my belief that quality of life is an important consideration in development planning. As Goulet explains:

> To determine what is good and what is bad development implies some qualitative view of life and society. . . . Unless one wishes to judge a society solely by the number of radios or miles of highway it has, he must appeal to qualitative indicators. (Goulet, 1971: 216)

It is also based on my conviction that men do not operate solely in terms of economic advantage. Karl Polanyi's economic analyses emphasized this (Polanyi, 1957: 249-50), and the work of economic anthropologists indicates that rural men, perhaps more than others, are motivated by (traditional) factors which have little to do with the maximization of material resources. Certainly this is substantiated by the communities studied here.

An alternative to the current regional development strategy must make the welfare of the people its central goal. Although some may think otherwise, I see nothing inherently socialistic or capitalistic about such a goal. This leaves open to question whose definition of "the welfare of the people" one accepts. My answer is "their own". Obviously uneducated fisherman, farmers and workers do not have the knowledge or expertise to devise a plan which will best reflect their goals and values. Only planning experts can *design* the plans needed. But the *choice of direction* that this planning takes should be left in the hands of the people. Since it is their lives which will be affected, their goals and values should be the ones upon which planning is based. Anything else is not planning but coercion and intimidation (Matthews, 1975b).

What is needed is an approach to regional development which works with the people of underdeveloped regions rather than without, against or even for them. Rural people are rational even if they are not motivated to maximize their economic advantage. The assumption which underlies the communities studied here is that people have reasons for their actions, even if these reasons are not immediately obvious to outsiders. In interviews the people of Small Harbour, Mountain Cove and Grande Terre made it clear that, from their point of view, it was perfectly rational for them to remain where they were. Planners must try to understand the rationality of the people and make their plans in accordance with it. In doing so they will be led to examine both the economic viability *and* the social vitality of the community, and to consider the values and goals of the people for whom they are planning. They must be trained to be aware of rural peoples' values and work within the existing community organizations and social structure.

The greatest obstacle to this type of regional planning is that planners and development workers may regard working with the people as little more than an exercise in public relations. Many people with technical expertise tend to assume that they have only to explain their proposals and others will see the inherent wisdom of them. But the goal that seems rational to the planners from their value orientation may have no meaning and make no sense whatsoever from the value position of the people. This situation is particularly likely to occur when people feel that their rights are threatened. No amount of logic or rational explanation on the part of planners is likely to convince them that such is not the case.

Any alternative to current development strategies must meet two further requirements. It must be job-oriented and it must, whenever possible, be resources-based. The primary need of underdeveloped regions is for jobs. The problem with most so-called propulsive industries is that they employ relatively few local workers at an enormous cost per workplace. What is needed is the development of smaller industries which are labour intensive and, at the same time, sufficiently technologically advanced to produce more goods than are needed for home consumption. The sale of this surplus would help to transform the local community from a near peasant economy into a market economy, and the cash income received would enable the region to become more economically viable.

One of the major advantages which any industry can have is to be based on local resources. The other is proximity to markets. It is rarely possible for any industry to be near both, since most resources are found in unpopulated hinterland areas while the major markets are in the metropolises. But while an industry which locates in the metropolis has the advantage of being near the markets, it must import raw materials. An industry which locates in an underdeveloped hinterland area can similarly maximize the advantage of being near the raw materials. Properly organized, this can actually give it an advantage over competitors in the urban centre, for it should cost less to ship a finished product than the larger amount of raw materials needed to produce the product. But this seldom happens since technological developments make it cheaper to ship raw materials in bulk form than to ship manufactured goods. Obviously more attention must be given to improving methods of transporting finished products if regional disparity is to be reduced. Unless this is accomplished, there seems to be little point in subsidizing industries to locate in under-developed areas.

One possible exception arises when residents of an area have a craft-like skill. A craft-based industry can locate in the area and utilize this "human resource". Perhaps the best known examples are the Swiss watch-makers and Czechoslovakian glass-blowers. Even areas which have limited natural resources can improve their situation if, through the help of development programmes, they develop the craftsmanship of local residents. However craft-based industries require the creation of national and world markets for fine quality crafted products rather than mass produced products.

It is ironical that traditional craft industries may succeed in fostering regional development in areas where modern, large scale industries have failed. Modern industrial developments usually fall into two categories (Blauner, 1967). On one hand there are "continuous process" industries such as petro-chemical complexes which are essentially machine tending enterprises employing only a few skilled men. The value of such industries in regional development is limited because they employ a small number of people at great cost. The second common type is the "assembly line" industry. While these industries employ large numbers of people with low skill levels, they produce a mass product which must be sold on the world market. Since most underdeveloped regions are some distance from major population centres, transportation costs alone usually mitigate against the success of these enterprises. They can succeed only as long as wages remain low enough to compensate for high transportation costs.

As an alternative to a strategy of heavy industrialization, small scale, local, resource based industries can overcome the problems encountered by both of these types of large scale industries. While he is essentially concerned with the development of third world countries, British economist E.F. Schumacher argues along these same lines. He advocates the development of "intermediate technology", which he defines as labour-intensive industry that is more advanced than the indigenous technology of an underdeveloped area, but less advanced than the highly capital-

intensive technology of modern industry (Schumacher, 1975: 163-205).
He sums up his strategy of development with four propositions:

1. that workplaces have to be created in the areas where the people are living now, and not primarily in metropolitan areas into which they tend to migrate.

2. that these workplaces must be, on average, cheap enough so that they can be created in large numbers without this calling for an unattainable level of capital formation and imports.

3. that the production methods employed must be relatively simple, so that the demands for high skills are minimized, not only in the production process itself but also in matters of organization, raw material supply, financing, marketing, and so forth.

4. that production should be mainly from local materials and mainly for local use.

(Ibid.: 175-176)

My conclusions differ slightly from his because the focus here is on regional development within an otherwise developed country rather than on the development of an undeveloped country. In contrast to Schumacher I believe that it is particularly important for local industries to produce a surplus of goods for outside sale. Only in this way can the cash be generated to enable the area to become self-sustaining. Secondly, the development of craft skills can provide an area with a major lever in eliminating regional economic differences. These suggestions are not just aimed at raising the standard of living, but at raising it to the point where the quality of life is as good as, if not better than that of other regions of the country. As the community studies show, many people do not define quality of life purely in materialistic terms. Many are willing to give up some of the modern amenities if they can live in their local communities.

In addition to Schumacher's work, there is a growing body of information to help planners formulate an alternative to the present growth centre development strategy. A relatively well-established tradition among British developers encourages the development of autonomous small communities. As one developer has described his work:

The primary objective is to offer another perfectly possible way of life to that in the cities. The first means to that end should be to encourage greater self-reliance among existing communities by seeking out and assisting all forms of local enterprise and by pro-

moting practical and fairly short-term projects which can give con-
fidence. Morale based on some economic activity is more important
than the perfect plan. (Grieve, 1972: 143)

In Canada, too, one well-known regional development economist has recently begun to urge that regional development must consider both economic *and* social factors.

> The main point is that in economic analysis, and particularly in
> regional analysis, explanations are offered in economic terms when
> in fact many of the elements are non-economic, cultural, social,
> political and psychological.

> In its widest sense, regional, social disparity is concerned with
> how people as individuals and as a community feel about their
> way of life. And this relates to differences in aspirations, wants,
> attitudes, satisfactions, motivation, behaviour, cultural traits, and
> involvement in community affairs. . . . In effect, regional social
> disparity relates not only to social circumstances which may differ
> from region to region *but also how people feel about these differences.*
> (Firestone, 1974: 213)

Nevertheless it would be a mistake to believe that there is a pat formula to follow in providing alternative programmes and policies of
regional and rural development that reflect the values and attitudes of
those who will be affected. Nor is there any quick way to develop programmes which do not undermine and destroy the culture and social
structure which many people wish to preserve. The development of
such policies must be slow and painstaking and may require considerable
prior insight into the communities to be affected. But through such
efforts our rural communities can become "better places" in which
to live.

COMMUNITY CHANGE SURVEY:
INTERVIEW QUESTIONNAIRE

Code Number: _____

_____

Present community: _____

Respondent's name: _____

If wife, include husband's first name

1. Interviewed:
    1. [ ] Male
    2. [ ] Female
    3. [ ] Husband and wife together
    4. [ ] Other _____

Specify

2. Marital status of respondent:
    1. [ ] Single
    2. [ ] Married
    3. [ ] Widowed
    4. [ ] Separated or divorced

3. Occupation: Husband or single man (*Also get for deceased husband*)
    1. [ ] Not Applicable (i.e. respondent single woman)
    2. [ ] Inshore fishing only (including longliner)
    3. [ ] Deepsea fishing only
    4. [ ] Other or combination of occupations (give all occupations and indicate which is main occupation)

    _____

4. Occupation: Wife or single woman (*Also get for deceased wife*)
    1. [ ] Not applicable
    2. [ ] Housewife only
    3. [ ] Other or combination of occupations (give all occupations and indicate which is main occupation)

    _____

5. Education of husband:
    Highest grade obtained: _____

    Other training: _____

6. Education of wife:
   Highest grade obtained: _____

   Other training: _____

7. Age of husband: _____

8. Age of wife: _____

Mobility of Husband or Single Man

Interviewer: *(a) If respondent a man, ask him to answer questions 9-13.*

(b) If respondent is a married woman and her husband is not present, ask her to provide the information in 9-13 about her husband.

(c) If respondent is a widowed or separated woman, ask her questions 9-11 only.

(d) If respondent is a single woman, skip to question 14.

9. Place of birth: Husband or single man (*Also get for deceased or separated husband*)
   1. [   ] Present community
   2. [   ] Other _____

                Community   Bay or Province

10. How long has husband (single man) lived here?
    1. [   ] All life
    2. [   ] Other _____

                       Number of years

11. Did husband (single man) ever live for longer than one month in any other community than this one?
    1. [   ] No (*Skip to Q.14*)
    2. [   ] Yes

Place	How long	When	What doing (occupation)	Why moved from there
____	_____	____	_____	_____

12. Does husband (single man) still think of any of these places as home?
    1. [   ] No
    2. [   ] Yes (specify community) _____

    Why? (or comment) _____

13. Does husband (single man) ever wish he were back in one of the other places that he has lived?
    1. [ ] No, not at all
    2. [ ] Yes, some
    3. [ ] Yes, very much

    If yes: Where? _____ Why?_____

Mobility of Wife or Single Woman

Interviewer: *(a) If respondent a woman, or if wife present when interviewing husband, ask her to answer questions 14-18.*

(b) If respondent is a married man and his wife is not present, ask him to provide the information in 14-18 about his wife.

(c) If respondent is a widowed or separated man, ask him questions 14-16 only

(d) If respondent is a single man, skip to question 19.

14. Place of birth: Wife or single woman (*Also get for deceased or separated wife*)
    1. [ ] Present community
    2. [ ] Other _____
       Community   Bay or Province

15. How long has wife (single woman) lived here?
    1. [ ] All life
    2. [ ] Other _____
       Number of years

16. Did wife (single woman) ever live for longer than one month in any other community than this one?
    1. [ ] No (*Skip to Q. 19*)
    2. [ ] Yes

Place	How long	When	What doing (occupation)	Why moved from there
___	_____	___	_____	_____

17. Does wife (single woman) still think of any of these places as home?
    1. [ ] No
    2. [ ] Yes (specify community) _____

    Why? (or comment) _____

18. Does wife (single woman) ever wish that she were back in one of the other places that she lived?
    1. [ ] No, not at all

2. [   ]   Yes, some
3. [   ]   Yes, very much

If yes: Where? _____ Why? _____

19. Who besides you (and your wife/husband) lives in this house?

Name	Age	Relation	Occupation	Grade	Other training	Marital status
———	——	———	————	——	———	———

Mobility of Children

Interviewer: If respondent single person, skip to question 30.

20. If have children at home: Have any of your children living here in this house ever lived in any other community
    1. [   ]   No *(Skip to Q. 22)*
    2. [   ]   Yes, but only with parents *(Skip to Q. 22)*
    3. [   ]   Yes, lived elsewhere on own

21. If lived elsewhere on own: Can you give me their names and where they lived?

Name	Where Lived	What doing (occupation)	Length of time there
——	——	———	————

22. Do you have any sons or daughters besides those that live with you in this house?
    1. [   ]   No *(Skip to Q. 28)*
    2. [   ]   Yes

If yes to question 22, ask questions 23-27.

23. Do any of these sons and daughters (who don't live in this house) live in present community.
    1. [   ]   No *(Skip to Q. 26)*
    2. [   ]   Yes

24. If yes to 23: What are their names and ages?

Name	Age	Occupation	Marital status	School grade	Other training
———	——	———	———	——	———

25. If yes to 23: Have any of them ever lived anywhere besides here for longer than a month?
    1. [   ]   No *(Skip to Q. 26)*
    2. [   ]   Yes, but only with parents *(Skip to Q. 26)*

3. [ ] Yes, lived elsewhere on own (*Give information below*)

Name	Where else lived	How long	When	What doing (occupation)
___	___	___	___	___

26. If yes to 23: Do you have any sons or daughters who are now living in other communities or cities?
    1. [ ] No (*Skip to Q. 28*)
    2. [ ] Yes

27. If yes to 23: What are their names and where are they living?

Name	Community	Time there	Age	What doing (occupation)	Marital status
___	___	___	___	___	___

School grade	Other training	Ever live here	When left	Why left
___	___	___	___	___

28. Did you have any children who have died?
    1. [ ] No (*Skip to Q. 30*)
    2. [ ] Yes

29. If yes to 28: How old were they and where were they living at the time of their death?

Name	Age	Where living	If elsewhere, ever live here
___	___	___	___

Housing and Life Style

30. Do you own your own house?
    1. [ ] Yes, own it outright
    2. [ ] Yes, but payments still being made
    3. [ ] No, paying rent
    4. [ ] No, living with relatives } Skip to Q.32
    5. [ ] No, other

31. If you own your own house, did you buy or build your house?
    1. [ ] Built house by himself
    2. [ ] Built house with help of friends and relatives (unpaid)
    3. [ ] Built house with paid helpers
    4. [ ] Had house built by other persons
    5. [ ] Bought house already finished from _____
       Relation of seller
    6. [ ] Inherited house from parent or relative
    7. [ ] Other _____

32. About how old is this house? _____
                                              Years old

33. How many rooms does this house have? _____

    How many bedrooms? _____

34. Are you satisfied with your present house?
    1. [ ] Yes, very satisfied
    2. [ ] Reasonably satisfied
    3. [ ] Have some complaints
    4. [ ] No, very dissatisfied

    What is it about your house that you like or dislike? _____

35. About how much would you expect to get for your house if you
    were to sell it here?
    1. [ ] Less than $1,000
    2. [ ] $1,000 to $1,999
    3. [ ] $2,000 to $2,999
    4. [ ] $3,000 to $3,999
    5. [ ] $4,000 to $4,999
    6. [ ] $5,000 to $5,999
    7. [ ] $6,000 to $7,999
    8. [ ] $8,000 to $9,999
    9. [ ] $10,000 and over $_____
    10. [ ] No market: Salvage value only $_____

36. How much is your house really worth (i.e. replacement value)?

    $ _____

37. If you were to build another house, about how much would you be
    willing to spend on it? (*Assume he is able to sell present house*)
    1. [ ] Less than $1,000
    2. [ ] $1,000 to $1,999
    3. [ ] $2,000 to $2,999
    4. [ ] $3,000 to $3,999
    5. [ ] $4,000 to $4,999
    6. [ ] $5,000 to $5,999
    7. [ ] $6,000 to $7,999
    8. [ ] $8,000 to $9,999
    9. [ ] $10,000 and over $_____

38. How is your house lighted?
    1. [ ] Oil or kerosene lamps
    2. [ ] Electricity from own power plant
    3. [ ] Electricity from power plant owned by other community
            member

4. [ ] Electricity from government owned power plant
5. [ ] Electricity from provincial hydro-power system
6. [ ] Other _____

39. How do you heat your house?
    1. [ ] Kitchen stove only
    2. [ ] Space heater only
    3. [ ] Space heater and kitchen stove
    4. [ ] Furnace
    5. [ ] Furnace and kitchen stove
    6. [ ] Furnace and space heater
    7. [ ] Furnace, kitchen stove and space heater
    8. [ ] Other _____

40. Do you have water piped into the house?
    1. [ ] No   If No: What source? _____
                 How far away? _____

    2. [ ] Yes

41. What kind of toilet do you have?
    1. [ ] Outdoor
    2. [ ] Chemical
    3. [ ] Flush

42. Which of the following do you have? (*Interviewer: Tick items owned*)
    1. [ ] Radio
    2. [ ] Television
    3. [ ] Electric kitchen range
    4. [ ] Oil kitchen range
    5. [ ] Refrigerator (electrical or mechanical)
    6. [ ] Washing machine (electrical or mechanical)
    7. [ ] Sewing machine
    8. [ ] Telephone
    9. [ ] Record player
    10. [ ] Vacuum cleaner
    11. [ ] Electric dryer
    12. [ ] Musical instrument _____
                                    Specify
    13. [ ] Gun

43. Do you own a car or truck?
    1. [ ] No
    2. [ ] Yes
    If yes: Type _____ Year_____

44. Do you or your wife/husband read any papers or magazines regularly?

1. [   ] No
2. [   ] Yes

If yes: Specify below which types

Weekend paper _____

Daily paper _____

News magazine _____

Religious magazine or paper _____

Fisherman's paper _____

Other _____

Community and Community Involvement

I would now like to ask you a few questions about life here in (present community).

45. Do you like living in (present community)?
    1. [   ] No
    2. [   ] Yes

    Comment _____

46. What would you say are the things you like *best* about living here? (*Interviewer: Tick where applicable and record verbatim answer below. Use numeric code for sequence*)
    1. [   ] Can make a living here
    2. [   ] Like the work I am doing
    3. [   ] Like the people in the community
    4. [   ] Like the availability of fresh game and produce
    5. [   ] Like the freedom and way of life
    6. [   ] Other

    Comment _____

47. What would you say are the things you like *least* (dislike) about living here? (*Interviewer: Tick where applicable and record verbatim answer below. Use numeric code for sequence*)
    1. [   ] No opportunity for children
    2. [   ] Poor educational system
    3. [   ] Difficulty of transportation
    4. [   ] Poor medical system
    5. [   ] Difficulties of communication
    6. [   ] Cannot get work here
    7. [   ] Isolation
    8. [   ] Other

    Comment _____

48. If you had a choice, where would you live?
    1. [　]　Right here
    2. [　]　Another place like this but with roads and better
    　　　　services
    3. [　]　Town
    4. [　]　City

Community _____ Why?_____

49. If have children living at home: Do your children like living here?
    1. [　]　Don't know or no answer (N/A)
    2. [　]　Children too small to decide
    3. [　]　No
    4. [　]　Some of them
    5. [　]　Yes

Comment _____

50. How many merchants are there in present community?
    1. [　]　None (*Skip to Q. 51*)
    2. [　]　One
    3. [　]　Two
    4. [　]　Three
    5. [　]　More than three _____
    　　　　　　　　　　　　　　　　Number

What are their names?

_____

51. If more than one merchant: Does one (or more) of these merchants
    have a bigger business than the other(s)?
    1. [　]　N/A or don't know
    2. [　]　Thinks they all do about the same business
    3. [　]　Yes

_____
    　　　　　　　　　Name(s)

52. Do you buy groceries from one merchant's store more than any other?
    1. [　]　N/A only one merchant
    2. [　]　N/A respondent is merchant
    3. [　]　No
    4. [　]　Yes _____
    　　　　　　　　　　　Name

_____
    　　　　　Community (if other)

53. How long have you done business with this merchant?
    1. [　]　N/A does not do business with only one merchant
    2. [　]　All life or as long as have been doing business

3. [ ] Over ten years, but not life
4. [ ] Over five years, but not ten
5. [ ] Over one year, but not five
6. [ ] Less than one year

Comment _____

54. Is the merchant you buy groceries from a relative?
    1. [ ] N/A
    2. [ ] No
    3. [ ] Yes _____
                           Relation

55. Do you shop for anything for your family or house in any other community?
    1. [ ] No
    2. [ ] Yes

If yes: What and where? _____

If respondent or husband is a fisherman, ask questions 54-59.
If not a fisherman, skip to question 60.

56. Where do you buy most of your fishing supplies and gear?

    Buy from: _____
             Merchant   Location   For how long?

    Where do you sell your catch?

    Sell to: _____
             Merchant   Location   For how long?

57. Are any of these people you do business with related to you?
    1. [ ] No
    2. [ ] Yes _____
                           Relation

58. What type of boat do you fish with?
    1. [ ] Dory
    2. [ ] Motor boat or trap skiff
    3. [ ] Longliner
    4. [ ] Dragger or trawler (offshore)
    5. [ ] Other _____

59. How many men do you fish with?
    1. [ ] None
    2. [ ] One
    3. [ ] Two
    4. [ ] Three
    5. [ ] Four

6. [   ] Five
7. [   ] More than five _____
                          Number

60. If fish inshore: What are the names of the men you fish with and are they related to you?

    Name   *Relation*

    _____   _____

61. If fish offshore: What company do you fish for?

    _____

    How did you get your job on this boat? _____

62. Do you or your wife/husband belong to any organizations, boards or committees? (*Interviewer: Probe for church groups, lodges, school board, road board, political groups, etc.*)

    Husband:
    1. [   ] N/A
    2. [   ] No
    3. [   ] Yes (give below)

    Organization   *Position*   *How often meet*   *How often attend*

    _____   _____   _____   _____

    Wife:
    1. [   ] N/A
    2. [   ] No
    3. [   ] Yes (give below)

    _____   _____   _____   _____

63. If your family was in difficulty or had a bad year, do you think you could depend on your friends and relatives in this community for help?
    1. [   ] Yes. All the time
    2. [   ] Yes. Most of the time (usually)
    3. [   ] Yes. In some circumstances (sometimes)
    4. [   ] Yes. But rarely
    5. [   ] No. Never

    Comment _____

64. If you were in need of someone to help you with some work you were doing, who would you be most likely to go to for help?
    1. [   ] N/A or don't know
    2. [   ] No one
    3. [   ] Depends on the situation

4. [ ] Name: _____

        Occupation (position): _____

        Relation (if any): _____

65. If you needed advice or information about something, who would you be most likely to go to for help?
    1. [ ] N/A or don't know
    2. [ ] No one
    3. [ ] Depends on the situation
    4. [ ] Name: _____

        Occupation (position): _____

        Relation (if any): _____

66. Who would you say are the community leaders in (present community)?
    1. [ ] Don't know or won't answer
    2. [ ] Answer (give below)

Name	*Occupation (position)*

67. Why do you think of these people as leaders?

68. How did they get to be leaders? *(Interviewer: Deal with each person given above separately)*

69. What things have the leaders here done? *(Probe for each leader)*

70. What things would you like to see the leaders here do differently?

71. Are there any young people here who are beginning to become leaders in the community? *(Probe for names, positions, occupations and activities)*

72. What have been the greatest changes you've experienced in your life here in (present community)? *(Probe and record verbatim)*

73. About how many families have moved out of (present community) in the last five years?

    1. [   ] None   5. [   ] Six to ten
    2. [   ] One   6. [   ] Eleven to fifteen
    3. [   ] Two or three   7. [   ] Sixteen to twenty
    4. [   ] Four or five   8. [   ] Over twenty _____

74. If families have left: Do you think that their leaving has had much effect on the community?

    1. [   ] No
    2. [   ] Yes

Why? (or comment) _____

75. Have any families moved into (present community) from the outside in the last five years?

    1. [   ] None (*Skip to Q. 70*)
    2. [   ] One
    3. [   ] Two or three
    4. [   ] Four or five
    5. [   ] Six to ten
    6. [   ] Eleven to fifteen
    7. [   ] Sixteen to twenty
    8. [   ] Over twenty _____
                             Number

76. If families have entered community: Do you think that by coming here they have had much effect on the community?

    1. [   ] No
    2. [   ] Yes

Why? (or comment) _____

77. Do you think that you live better or worse today than you lived fifteen or twenty years ago?

    1. [   ] A lot better
    2. [   ] Somewhat better
    3. [   ] About the same
    4. [   ] Somewhat worse
    5. [   ] A lot worse

Why? (or comment) _____

78. Would you say that this community has improved or declined in the last fifteen or twenty years?

    1. [   ] Improved
    2. [   ] Declined
    3. [   ] No change

Why do you think it has improved or declined? _____

79. How would you compare the way you live here with the way people live in nearby growth centre?
    1. [ ] A lot better here
    2. [ ] Somewhat better here
    3. [ ] About the same here
    4. [ ] Somewhat worse here
    5. [ ] A lot worse here

    (*Interviewer: Probe for attitude toward growth centre*)

    Comment _____

80. How are the chances for children in (present community) to get an education these days?
    1. [ ] Good
    2. [ ] Medium
    3. [ ] Poor

    Comment _____

81. Do you feel that young people when they finish school should stay here, or should they try and make a living somewhere else?
    1. [ ] N/A or don't know
    2. [ ] It's up to them
    3. [ ] Should stay here
    4. [ ] Should leave

    Why? (or comment) _____

82. If have school age children: Would you like to see your own children stay here when they finish school or would you like to see them go somewhere else?
    1. [ ] N/A
    2. [ ] Up to them
    3. [ ] All stay here
    4. [ ] Some stay and others go
    5. [ ] All leave

    Who and why?; Stay or go? _____

83. Have you and your wife/husband ever thought of leaving here yourself?
    1. [ ] No
    2. [ ] Yes

    Why? (or comment)_____

84. What do you think you/your husband could do to make a better living in this community?

_____

85. If the people here were to work together as a group, is there anything they could do so that people here could make a better living or be better off?

_____

86. How do you think the government could help the people here so that they could make a better living or be better off?

_____

87. Have you ever heard of the government's resettlement programme? (*Ask also as centralization and "shifting money"*)
    1. [ ] No (*Skip to Q. 84*)
    2. [ ] Yes

88. How did you hear about the resettlement programme? (*Use multiple check*)
    1. [ ] N/A or don't know
    2. [ ] Radio or T.V.
    3. [ ] Paper or magazine
    4. [ ] From welfare officer
    5. [ ] From community development worker
    6. [ ] From politician
    7. [ ] From merchant
    8. [ ] From conversations in the community
    9. [ ] Other _____

89. Do you think that the resettlement programme is a good idea?
    1. [ ] Don't know
    2. [ ] Yes, good idea
    3. [ ] No, against it

    Why? (or comment) _____

90. Is there much talk about the resettlement programme in present community?
    1. [ ] No
    2. [ ] Yes

    Comment _____

91. Has anyone ever tried to convince you to move under the resettlement programme?
    1. [ ] No

2. [　] Yes _____

                     Name   Position

Comment _____

92. Would you say that the people here are in favour of or against re-settlement?
    1. [　] Don't know or N/A
    2. [　] Against it
    3. [　] In favour of it

Why? (or comment) _____

93. Why do you think the government has developed the resettlement programme?
    1. [　] Don't know or N/A
    2. [　] It's cheaper to move us
    3. [　] To give us better services
    4. [　] Other

Comment _____

General Information

94. What religious denomination do you and your wife/husband belong to?

Husband:
    1. [　] N/A (respondent unmarried, widowed or divorced woman)
    2. [　] Anglican
    3. [　] Roman Catholic
    4. [　] United Church
    5. [　] Salvation Army
    6. [　] Pentecostal
    7. [　] Other _____
                                   Specify

Wife:
    1. [　] N/A (respondent, unmarried, widowed or divorced man)
    2. [　] Anglican
    3. [　] Roman Catholic
    4. [　] United Church
    5. [　] Salvation Army
    6. [　] Pentecostal
    7. [　] Other _____
                                   Specify

95. Does your religious denomination have a church here in (present community)?

Husband: Wife:
   1. [ ] No   1. [ ] No
   2. [ ] Yes   2. [ ] Yes

96. Does your religious denomination have a clergyman or priest living in (present community)?

Husband: Wife:
   1. [ ] No   1. [ ] No
   2. [ ] Yes   2. [ ] Yes

If no: Where is the clergyman that serves here stationed?

_____

97. If no resident clergyman: How often does the clergyman or priest visit here?

Husband: Wife: if different religion
   1. [ ] Don't know or N/A
   2. [ ] Daily
   3. [ ] Several times a week
   4. [ ] Once a week
   5. [ ] Once every two weeks
   6. [ ] Once every three weeks
   7. [ ] Once a month
   8. [ ] Less often _____
                                       Specify

98. Have you or your wife/husband ever belonged to a different religious denomination?

Husband:
   1. [ ] N/A
   2. [ ] No
   3. [ ] Yes _____
                                       Specify

Wife:
   1. [ ] N/A
   2. [ ] No
   3. [ ] Yes _____
                                         Specify

99. Has husband been employed at any job other than main occupation in the past twelve months?
   1. [ ] N/A
   2. [ ] No
   3. [ ] Yes _____
                                       Specify

100. Has husband been without work for any period in the last twelve months?
    1. [   ] N/A
    2. [   ] No
    3. [   ] Yes _____
                                  Length of time

101. Do you or your wife/husband have any brothers or sisters who live here in (present community)?
    1. [   ] No
    2. [   ] Yes

Name	Sibling of h/w	What doing (occupation)	Approximate age	Marital status
_____	____	_____	_____	____

102. Do you or your wife/husband have any brothers or sisters who used to live here but have now left?
    1. [   ] No
    2. [   ] Yes

Name	Sibling of h/w	Where living	What doing (occupation)	Approximate age	Marital status
____	___	_____	_____	_____	___

103. Do you or your wife/husband have any brothers or sisters who used to live here but have died here or elsewhere?
    1. [   ] No
    2. [   ] Yes

Where were they living at the time of their death?

Name	Sibling of h/w	Where living
_____	_____	_____

104. Do you know of any family in (present community) who is wanting to leave here?
    1. [   ] No
    2. [   ] Yes *(Probe for name, occupation and how know)*

105. Are parents of husband alive?
    1. [   ] No
    2. [   ] Yes, both
    3. [   ] Yes, one of them _____

If yes: Do they live in (present community)?

    1. [   ] Yes
    2. [   ] No _____
                              Specify where

106. Are parents of wife alive?
     1. [   ] No
     2. [   ] Yes, both
     3. [   ] Yes, one of them _____

     If yes: Do they live in (present community)?
     1. [   ] Yes
     2. [   ] No _____
                                        Specify where

107. Have you or your wife/husband been to any other community in the past 12 months?

     Husband:
     1. [   ] No
     2. [   ] Yes

     If yes:

     Where   *How long there*   *Why there*
     _____   _____   _____

     Wife:
     1. [   ] No
     2. [   ] Yes

     If yes:

     Where   *How long there*   *Why there*
     _____   _____   _____

COMMUNITY SATISFACTION INDEX

Code Number: _____

_____

Respondent's name: _____
(If wife, include husband's first name)

Present community: _____

I would now like to ask you a few questions about how you feel about living in this place. I am going to read you some statements and I am going to ask you whether you *agree or disagree* with them. To each statement you have five choices you can make. (*Interviewer: Explain the five choices.*)

For example, if I asked you, "Do you think this is a good place to bring up children?", which of these answers would you give:

(1) Strongly agree (2) Agree (3) Uncertain (4) Disagree (5) Strongly disagree

	Strongly agree	Agree	Uncertain	Disagree	Strongly disagree
1. No one who lives here seems to care how this community looks.	1	2	3	4	5
2. The future of this community looks very good.	5	4	3	2	1
3. This community is not located in a very good place.	1	2	3	4	5
4. You can't say much good about a place this size.	1	2	3	4	5
5. There are very few families you would care to marry into in this community.	1	2	3	4	5
6. The people just can't get together on anything here.	1	2	3	4	5
7. This place will never seem like home to me.	1	2	3	4	5
8. The leaders here are generally hard working, good, capable people.	5	4	3	2	1

	Strongly agree	Agree	Uncertain	Disagree	Strongly disagree
9. People who live here have to do without a good many conveniences.	1	2	3	4	5
10. This community usually has to put up with poor teachers.	1	2	3	4	5
11. Almost everyone here is ready and willing to work.	5	4	3	2	1
12. You just can't get good medical care here.	1	2	3	4	5
13. This community has to put up with poor school buildings and facilities.	1	2	3	4	5
14. You can buy things here at a reasonable price.	5	4	3	2	1
15. The people here as a whole mind their own business.	5	4	3	2	1
16. The chances for a person to better himself here are pretty small.	1	2	3	4	5
17. Most of the nearby communities are no better than here.	5	4	3	2	1
18. A person who is down and out is not likely to receive much help here.	1	2	3	4	5
19. Real friends are hard to find here.	1	2	3	4	5
20. Everyone here has a say in deciding how things should be run.	5	4	3	2	1
21. Most people enjoy living here.	5	4	3	2	1

REFERENCES

All of the following references have been cited in the text of this book.

APEC 1972. *The Atlantic Economy: Sixth Annual Review.* Halifax: Atlantic Provinces Economic Council.

Blauner, Robert. 1967. *Alienation and Freedom.* Phoenix Books. Chicago: University of Chicago Press.

Brewis, T.N. 1969. *Regional Economic Policies in Canada.* Toronto: Macmillan Company of Canada.

Buckley, Helen and Eva Tihanyi. 1967. *Canadian Policies for Rural Adjustment: A Study of the Economic Impact of ARDA, PFRA and MMRA.* Special Study, no. 7. Ottawa: Economic Council of Canada.

Copes, Parzival. 1972. *The Resettlement of Fishing Communities in Newfoundland.* Ottawa: Canadian Council on Rural Development.

Finn, D.B. 1965. *Report of the Atlantic Salt Fish Commission.* Ottawa: Department of Trade and Commerce.

Firestone, O.J. 1974. Regional Economic and Social Disparity. In *Regional Economic Development,* ed. O.J. Firestone, pp. 205-67. Ottawa: Editions de l'université d'Ottawa.

Francis, J.P. and N.G. Pillai. 1972. *Regional Development and Regional Policy: Some Issues and Recent Canadian Experience.* Ottawa: Department of Regional Economic Expansion of Canada.

Gans, Herbert J. 1972. The Positive Functions of Poverty. *American Journal of Sociology,* vol. 78, no. 2: 275-89.

Glaser, Barney G. and Anselm L. Strauss. 1967. *The Discovery of Grounded Theory: Strategies for Qualitative Research.* Chicago: Aldine Publishing.

Gouldner, Alvin W. 1970. *The Coming Crisis of Western Sociology.* New York: Basic Books.

Goulet, Denis. 1971. *The Cruel Choice: A New Concept in the Theory of Development.* New York: Atheneum.

Great Britain. 1933. *Report of the Newfoundland Royal Commission.* London: H.M. Stationery Office.

Grieve, Sir Robert. 1972. Problems and Objectives in the Highlands and Islands. In *The Remoter Rural Areas of Britain,* ed. J. Ashton and W.H. Long, pp. 130-45. Edinburgh: Oliver and Boyd.

Iverson, Noel and Ralph Matthews. 1968. *Communities in Decline: An Examination of Household Resettlement in Newfoundland.* Newfoundland Social and Economic Studies, no. 6. St. John's: Institute of Social and Economic Research, Memorial University.

Lamarre, Nicole. 1973. Kinship and Inheritance Patterns in a French New-
foundland Village. In *Communities and Culture in French Canada,* ed.
Gerald L. Gold and Marc-Adelard Trembley, pp. 142-153. Toronto:
Holt, Rinehart and Winston of Canada.

Lane, Honorable C.M. 1967. Centralizing our Population. In *The Book
of Newfoundland,* ed. Joseph R. Smallwood, vol. 3. St. John's Newfoundland Book Publishers (1967).

Lewis, David. 1972. *Louder Voices: The Corporate Welfare Bums.* Toronto: James, Lewis and Samuel.

Mandel, Ernest. 1974. *Capitalism and Regional Disparity.* Toronto: New
Hogtown Press.

Martin, Anne. 1974. Up-Along: Newfoundland Families in Hamilton.
Unpublished M.A. Thesis, McMaster University.

Martindale, Don.
   1962 *Social Life and Cultural Change.* Princeton: Van Nostrand.
   1963 The Formation and Destruction of Communities. In *Explora-
      tions in Social Change,* ed. G.K. Zollschan and W. Hirsch, pp.
      61-87. Boston: Houghton Mifflin.
   1966 *Institutions, Organizations, and Mass Society.* Boston: Hough-
      ton Mifflin.

Matthews, Ralph.
   1970 Communities in Transition: An Examination of Government
      Initiated Community Migration in Rural Newfoundland. Un-
      published M.A. Thesis, University of Minnesota.
   1974 Perspectives on Recent Newfoundland Politics. *Journal of
      Canadian Studies,* vol. IX, no. 2: 20-35.
   1975a The Smallwood Legacy: Newfoundland Social and Economic
      Development, 1949-1972. Unpublished manuscript.
   1975b Ethical Issues in Policy Research. *Canadian Public Policy,* vol. 1,
      no. 2: 204-16.

Newfoundland. 1967. *Report of the Royal Commission on the Economic
State and Prospects of Newfoundland and Labrador.* St. John's.

Newfoundland. 1970a. *A Social and Economic Development Program
for Newfoundland and Labrador in the 1970s.* Prepared by the
Honourable William N. Rowe, Minister of Community and Social
Development. St. John's.

Newfoundland. 1970b. *The Historic Coast: A Proposal for Integrated
Development of the Great Northern Peninsula Centered Upon the
Proposed Gros Morne National Park.* St. John's: Department of
Mines, Agriculture and Resources.

Newfoundland. 1972. *Report of the Royal Commission on Labour Legislation in Newfoundland and Labrador.* St. John's.

Noel, S.R.J. 1971. *Politics in Newfoundland.* Toronto: University of Toronto Press.

OECD 1969. *Multidisciplinary Aspects of Regional Development.* Paris: Development Centre of the Organization for Economic Co-operation and Development.

Perroux, Francois. 1955. Notes sur la notion de 'pole de croissance'. *Economic Appliquee,* janvier-juin. Translated as Notes on the Concept of Growth Roles. In *Regional Economics,* ed. D. McKee, R.D. Dean, W.H. Leahy. New York: Free Press, 1970.

Phidd, R.W. 1974. Regional Development Policy. In *Issues in Canadian Public Policy,* ed. G. Bruce Doern and Seymour Wilson, pp. 166-202. Toronto: Macmillan Company of Canada.

Poetschke, L.E. 1971. Regional Planning for Depressed Rural Areas: The Canadian Experience. In *Poverty in Canada,* ed. John Harp and John Hofley, pp. 270-81. Scarborough: Prentice Hall of Canada.

Polanyi, Karl. 1957. *The Great Transformation.* Boston: Beacon Press.

Robb, A.L. and R.E. Robb. 1969. *A Cost-Benefit Analysis of the Newfoundland Resettlement Program.* St. John's: Institute of Social and Economic Research, Memorial University.

Robertson, Heather. 1973. *Grass Roots.* Toronto: James Lewis and Samuel.

Rogers, J.D. 1911. *Newfoundland.* A Historical Geography of the British Colonies, vol. 5, part 4. Oxford: Clarendon Press.

Rostow, W.W. 1956. The Take-Off into Self-Sustained Growth. *The Economic Journal,* vol. 11, March: 25-48. Reprinted in *Two Worlds of Change: Readings in Economic Development,* ed. Otto Feinstein. Garden City: Anchor Books, 1964.

Schumacher, E.F. 1975. *Small is Beautiful: Economics as if People Mattered.* New York: Harper and Row.

Smallwood, Joseph R. 1973. *I Chose Canada.* Toronto: Macmillan Company of Canada.

Thahane, T. 1967. Population Growth and Shifts in Newfoundland. Unpublished B. Comm. Thesis, Memorial University.

Thomas, Morgan D. 1972. Growth Pole Theory: An Examination of Some of its Basic Concepts. In *Growth Centres in Regional Economic Development,* ed. Niles M. Hansen, pp. 50-81. New York: Free Press.

Thompson, Frederick F. 1961. *The French Shore Problem in Newfoundland: An Imperial Study.* Canadian Studies in History and Government, no. 2. Toronto: University of Toronto Press.

Newspapers

The Daily News, St. John's, Newfoundland
The Evening Telegram, St. John's, Newfoundland
The Newfoundland Bulletin, Government of Newfoundland: St. John's, Newfoundland